A FIRST COURSE IN
FORMAL LANGUAGE THEORY

COMPUTER SCIENCE TEXTS

COMPUTER SCIENCE TEXTS

A First Course in Formal Language Theory

V. J. RAYWARD-SMITH
MA, PhD

Senior Lecturer in Computing
University of East Anglia
Norwich NR4 7TJ, UK

BLACKWELL SCIENTIFIC PUBLICATIONS

OXFORD LONDON EDINBURGH

BOSTON MELBOURNE

© 1983 by
Blackwell Scientific Publications
Editorial offices:
Osney Mead, Oxford, OX2 OEL
8 John Street, London, WC1N 2ES
9 Forrest Road, Edinburgh, EH1 2QH
52 Beacon Street, Boston
    Massachusetts 02108, USA
99 Barry Street, Carlton
    Victoria 3053, Australia

First published 1983

DISTRIBUTORS

USA
  Blackwell Mosby Book Distributors
  11830 Westline Industrial Drive
  St Louis, Missouri 63141

Canada
  Blackwell Mosby Book Distributors
  120 Melford Drive, Scarborough
  Ontario, M1B 2X4

Australia
  Blackwell Scientific Book Distributors
  31 Advantage Road, Highett
  Victoria 3190

British Library
Cataloguing in Publication Data

Rayward-Smith, V.J.
  A first course in formal language theory.
  1. Linguistics   2. Languages—Philosophy
  I. Title
  401   P121

ISBN 0-632-01176-9

Photoset by Thomson Press (India) Ltd., New Delhi,
and printed and bound in Great Britain at the Alden Press, Oxford

To my family

A book that furnishes no quotations is, **me judice**, *no book — it is a plaything.*

T. L. PEACOCK: *Crotchet Castle*

Contents

Preface, ix
Introduction, xi

1   Mathematical Prerequisites, 1

sets; cardinality and countability; products of sets; graphs and trees; strings.

2   An Introduction to Grammars, 15

syntax charts and BNF; phrase structure grammars; context-free grammars; parsing arithmetic expressions; the empty string in CFGs.

3   Regular Languages I, 29

regular grammars; finite state automata; finite state automata with ε-moves.

4   Regular Languages II, 45

regular expressions; minimization; algorithms for regular grammars.

5   Context-free Languages, 55

Chomsky Normal Form; Greibach Normal Form; CFLs as solutions of equations.

6   Pushdown Automata, 70

nondeterministic pushdown automata; NPDAs as acceptors for CFLs; deterministic PDAs.

7   Top-down Parsing, 85

$LL(k)$ grammars; recursive descent.

8   Bottom-up Parsing, 102

simple precedence grammars; $LR(0)$ grammars; $LR(1)$ grammars; theoretical considerations.

Index, 121

Preface

Formal language theory is often a stumbling block for computer science undergraduates because of its heavy dependence upon notation. The subject cannot be avoided, however, because any self-respecting computer scientist must have a good understanding of compiling and this, in turn, relies heavily on the theory of formal languages. This book is aimed at first- and second-year undergraduates with the intention of providing enough background material to ensure that the reader will be adequately prepared for any course in compiling techniques. For this reason, concentration is centred, almost exclusively, on regular and context-free grammars.

Most textbooks in this field are aimed at third-year and postgraduate readers. Such books are more thorough in their approach but have proved daunting to many students. I have tried to make this text as simple as possible without sacrificing all rigour. In the early chapters, I go through the proofs carefully and in detail to show how formal proofs are constructed. The proof technique is nearly always induction and as the reader becomes accustomed to the format so less and less detail is included. By the end of the book, most proofs are in outline only and the emphasis has become increasingly practical. The interdependence of the chapters is illustrated by Fig. 0.1.

By the end of the second year of a 3-year course in computing, the student should have covered the majority of the material in this book. A first-year course might use just Chapters 1, 2, 3 and 5 although many

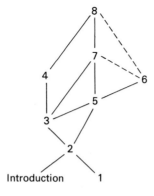

Figure 0.1

universities will also aim to include some material from Chapters 4 and 6. If a university offers a course specifically in formal language theory then the material in this book can be taught in about twenty one-hour lectures.

Much of the motivation for writing this book came from a group of undergraduates at the University of California at Santa Barbara, U.S.A. Whilst on sabbatical at that university, I taught a one-semester course on formal language theory to a class comprising largely of juniors. I am grateful for their enthusiasm and for the help and encouragement that I received from the department and from my own university during the preparation of this text. In particular, I would like to thank Dr G. P. McKeown (East Anglia) for his comments on draft versions and Theodora Potter (Santa Barbara) for her excellent typing of the manuscript.

V. J. Rayward-Smith

Introduction

When starting upon a study of languages, whether formal or not, we all share one great advantage. We are already experts in one language—the language in which we communicate with one another. Whether our natural language is English, French, Spanish, or whatever, we have mastered a valuable skill and will continue developing it for the rest of our lives. As well as being proficient in one or more natural language, most of us will be familiar with, and possibly expert in, various programming languages such as ALGOL68, PASCAL, FORTRAN or BASIC. These languages are used to write programs and hence to communicate with the computer. No doubt, like me, you will have noticed that your computer is particularly poor at understanding the intended meaning of your programs! While in natural language we can generally communicate quite adequately with one another in ill-structured and often incomplete sentences, once we have to communicate with the computer the situation changes. Our programs have to adhere rigorously to stringent rules and even minor deviations are rejected as being incorrect.

Ideally, any sentence in any language should be correct both *semantically* (i.e. have the correct meaning) and *syntactically* (i.e. have the correct grammatical structure). In spoken English, sentences are often syntactically incorrect but nevertheless convey the necessary semantics. In programming, however, it is essential that syntax is correct in order to convey any semantics whatsoever.

When we study the semantics of a sentence, we are studying its meaning. All the sentences below have the same semantic interpretation, i.e. all have the same meaning.

> The man hits the dog.
> The dog is hit by the man.
> L'homme frappe le chien.

The study of syntax is the study of grammar, i.e. of the structure of sentences. The English sentence

> The man hits the dog

can be *parsed*, i.e. resolved into component grammatical parts, as

$$\underbrace{\text{The man}}_{\langle\text{noun phrase}\rangle} \quad \underbrace{\text{hits}}_{\langle\text{verb phrase}\rangle} \quad \underbrace{\text{the dog}}_{\langle\text{noun phrase}\rangle}$$

and any sentence of this form is syntactically valid in English.

We could describe a particular collection of such simple sentences in English using the following rules.

⟨SIMPLE SENTENCE⟩::=⟨NOUN PHRASE⟩
⟨VERB PHRASE⟩⟨NOUN PHRASE⟩
⟨NOUN PHRASE⟩::=⟨ARTICLE⟩⟨NOUN⟩
⟨NOUN⟩::=CAR
⟨NOUN⟩::=MAN
⟨NOUN⟩::=DOG
⟨ARTICLE⟩::=THE
⟨ARTICLE⟩::=A
⟨VERB PHRASE⟩::=HITS
⟨VERB PHRASE⟩::=EATS

These rules are written in BNF (Backus–Naur Form), which is a notation commonly used to describe the syntax of programming languages. We will be discussing this notation in detail in Chapter 2.

In our example, a ⟨SIMPLE SENTENCE⟩ is defined as a ⟨NOUN PHRASE⟩ followed by a ⟨VERB PHRASE⟩ followed by a ⟨NOUN PHRASE⟩. The two ⟨NOUN PHRASE⟩s must be expanded to be an ⟨ARTICLE⟩ followed by a ⟨NOUN⟩. Choosing to expand the first ⟨ARTICLE⟩ as THE, the first ⟨NOUN⟩ as MAN, the ⟨VERB PHRASE⟩ as HITS, the second ⟨ARTICLE⟩ as THE and finally the last ⟨NOUN⟩ as DOG shows that the sentence THE MAN HITS THE DOG is one of our simple sentences. All of this can be neatly summarized by using what is termed a derivation tree, as in Fig. 0.2.

In fact, the definition of ⟨SIMPLE SENTENCE⟩ we have given results in 72 different derivable sentences. Although all of them are syntactically

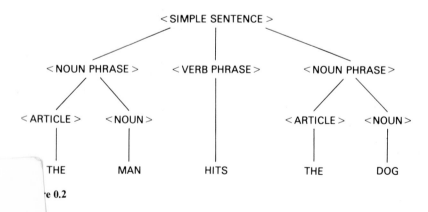

e 0.2

correct according to our definition, some of them appear not to have a sensible semantic interpretation, i.e. not to make sense. One seemingly nonsensical sentence is THE CAR EATS THE MAN. This illustrates the fact that a syntactically correct sentence in English need not necessarily make sense.

Now, consider the following sentence (which is not derivable from ⟨SIMPLE SENTENCE⟩).

THEY ARE FLYING PLANES

One parse of this sentence is

$$\underbrace{\text{THEY}}_{\langle\text{PRONOUN}\rangle} \quad \underbrace{\text{ARE}}_{\langle\text{VERB}\rangle} \quad \underbrace{\underbrace{\text{FLYING}}_{\langle\text{ADJECTIVE}\rangle} \quad \underbrace{\text{PLANES}}_{\langle\text{NOUN}\rangle}}_{\langle\text{NOUN PHRASE}\rangle}$$

This would suggest that THEY are PLANES in the sky that are flying at the moment. An alternative parse would be

$$\underbrace{\text{THEY}}_{\langle\text{PRONOUN}\rangle} \quad \underbrace{\text{ARE FLYING}}_{\langle\text{VERB}\rangle} \quad \underbrace{\text{PLANES}}_{\langle\text{NOUN}\rangle}$$

and this would imply a completely different semantic interpretation where THEY would refer to whoever is currently at the control of the PLANES. In this example, syntax analysis has been an aid to semantic interpretation. Although this is a rather contrived example and does not illustrate a common phenomenon in natural language, it is illustrative of an important concept in computing. A crucial stage in the compilation of a computer program is the parsing of that program as an essential step towards its semantic interpretation. For this reason, the study of syntax is a necessary part of computer science. Much of this book is devoted to examining how programming languages are defined using grammars and to the investigation of the properties of these grammars. A good understanding of grammars is a must for any computer scientist while the structures we investigate should also excite any mathematician. In fact, although this book is directed at potential computer scientists who are still at a relatively early stage in their studies, formal language theory is often regarded as a branch of mathematics and much of the work is of just such a nature. For a more advanced approach I strongly recommend *Introduction to Automata Theory, Languages and Computation* by J. E. Hopcroft and J. D. Ullman, published by Addison-Wesley, Reading, Mass.

Chapter 1

Mathematical Prerequisites

Mathematics possesses not only truth, but supreme beauty—a beauty cold and austere, like that of sculpture.

LORD BERTRAND RUSSELL
The Study of Mathematics

In this chapter, we will survey the mathematics required to understand the rest of this book. If this material is new to you, you should study it carefully and make sure you understand all of the concepts. You might like to supplement your reading with Chapters 1, 2 and 5 of the text by G.P. McKeown and V.J. Rayward-Smith, *Mathematics for Computing* published by Macmillan, London. If, on the other hand, the material is not new to you, this chapter can be skipped through quickly just to ascertain the notation that we are going to adopt.

SETS

A *set* is simply a collection of objects without repetition. Each object in a set is called an *element* of that set. If the number of such elements is not too large then the set can be specified by listing its elements. For example, if D denotes the set of days of the week, then

$$D = \{\text{Monday, Tuesday, Wednesday, Thursday, Friday,}$$
$$\text{Saturday, Sunday}\}.$$

The elements of a set defined in this way are separated by commas and surrounded by the special brackets, { and }. Generally, there is no implied ordering of the elements of a set, so we could equally well have defined

$$D = \{\text{Monday, Wednesday, Friday, Thursday, Sunday,}$$
$$\text{Tuesday, Saturday}\}.$$

If an element, x, is a member of a set, A, then we write $x \in A$ (read: x in A) and if x is not an element of A, we write $x \notin A$ (read: x not in A). Thus,

Monday $\in D$

and

Kippers $\notin D$

1

Often, however, a set has a large number of elements and perhaps even an infinite number of elements. In such cases the definition of the set cannot be given by listing all its elements and some *defining property* has to be specified. An element, x, is then in the set providing x satisfies the defining property. A suitable defining property for the set D is

'x is a day of the week'.

So, we could write

$$D = \{x \,|\, x \text{ is a day of the week}\}$$

i.e. D consists of all elements, x, that satisfy the defining property. As another example,

$$P = \{x \,|\, x \text{ is a prime number}\}$$

defines an infinite set of integers.

When defining a set in this way, care has to be taken to specify the elements under consideration as the *universe* (*of discourse*). For example, if

$$X = \{x \,|\, x > 2\}$$

then the precise nature of X can only be determined given the values which x might take. For example, if x could only range over the positive integers, X would be a different set from the case where x could range over all numbers. In the former case $2.1 \notin X$ but in the latter $2.1 \in X$. Every set under discussion will have all its elements contained in some specified universe, $\mathcal{U}$. Suitable universes in which X might be defined are the integers, the reals, the positive integers, the positive reals, etc.

A particularly important set is the *empty set*. This set contains no elements and is denoted by $\varnothing$ or $\{\ \}$.

We say a set A is a *subset* of a set B, written $A \subset B$, if every element of A is a member of the set B. If A is not a subset of B, we write $A \not\subset B$. Thus

$$\{1,2,4\} \subset \{1,2,3,4,5\}$$

and

$$\{2,4,6\} \not\subset \{1,2,3,4,5\}.$$

It follows from the definition that for all sets, A

$$A \subset \mathcal{U}$$

and

$$\varnothing \subset A.$$

sets A and B are said to be equal, written $A = B$, provided $A \subset B$ A. Thus

$$\{1,2,3,4\} = \{2,1,4,3\}$$

but

$$\{1,2,3,4\} \neq \{2,1,3,5\}.$$

Clearly, $A = B$ iff[1] A and B contain precisely the same elements.

The basic operations on sets are the unary[2] operation, complement ($'$) and the binary[3] operations union ($\cup$), intersection ($\cap$) and difference ($\backslash$). These operations are defined as follows: if A, B are sets then

$A' = \{x \mid x \notin A\}$ consists of all elements in the universe which are not in A;

$A \cup B = \{x \mid x \in A$ or $x \in B\}$ consists of all elements in either A or B;

$A \cap B = \{x \mid x \in A$ and $x \in B\}$ consists of all elements in both A and B;

$A \backslash B = \{x \mid x \in A$ but $x \notin B\}$ consists of all elements in A but not in B.

For example, if $\mathcal{U} = \{0,1,2,3,4,5,6,7,8,9\}$, $A = \{0,1,3,5\}$ and $B = \{2,3,5\}$, then

$$A' = \{2,4,6,7,8,9\},$$
$$A \cup B = \{0,1,2,3,5\},$$
$$A \cap B = \{3,5\}$$
$$A \backslash B = \{0,1\},$$

and

$$B \backslash A = \{2\}.$$

Note that $\cup$ and $\cap$ are both *associative* operations, i.e. for all sets A, B and C

$$(A \cup B) \cup C = A \cup (B \cup C)$$

and

$$(A \cap B) \cap C = A \cap (B \cap C).$$

Difference, however, is not associative. Similarly, $\cup$ and $\cap$ are both *commutative*, i.e.

$$A \cup B = B \cup A$$

---

[1] A standard abbreviation for 'if and only if'.
[2] Unary because the operation takes just one operand.
[3] Binary because the operation takes two operands.

and

$$A \cap B = B \cap A, \text{ for all sets } A, B$$

but \ is not. These and other properties of sets are summarized in Theorem 1.1.

Theorem 1.1. Properties of sets

For all sets A, B, C in the universe, $\mathcal{U}$:

1 Associative laws $\qquad (A \cup B) \cup C = A \cup (B \cup C)$
        and $\qquad\quad (A \cap B) \cap C = A \cap (B \cap C)$;

2 Commutative laws $\qquad A \cup B = B \cup A$
        and $\qquad\quad A \cap B = B \cap A$;

3 Complement laws $\qquad A \cup A' = \mathcal{U}$
        and $\qquad\quad A \cap A' = \emptyset$;

4 Idempotency laws $\qquad A \cup A = A$
        and $\qquad\quad A \cap A = A$;

5 Identity laws $\qquad A \cup \phi = A$
        and $\qquad\quad A \cap \mathcal{U} = A$;

6 Zero laws $\qquad A \cup \mathcal{U} = \mathcal{U}$
        and $\qquad\quad A \cap \emptyset = \emptyset$;

7 Involution law $\qquad (A')' = A$;

8 De Morgan's laws $\qquad (A \cup B)' = A' \cap B'$
        and $\qquad\quad (A \cap B)' = A' \cup B'$;

9 Distributivity laws $\qquad A \cup (B \cap C) = (A \cup B) \cap (A \cup C)$
        and $\qquad\quad A \cap (B \cup C) = (A \cap B) \cup (A \cap C)$.

Since union is associative, we can write $A \cup B \cup C$ and know that however it is evaluated, the same answer will result. Extending this argument, we can write $A_1 \cup A_2 \cup \ldots \cup A_n$ for any sets $A_1, A_2, \ldots, A_n$ without fear of misinterpretation. A common notation for such a union will be

$$\bigcup_{i=1}^{n} A_i.$$

···ly we write

for $A_1 \cap A_2 \cap \ldots \cap A_n$.

We say two sets A, B are *disjoint* if they have no elements in common. A convenient way of expressing this fact is to write $A \cap B = \emptyset$.

CARDINALITY AND COUNTABILITY

If A has a finite number of elements, it is called a *finite set* and if it has an infinite number of elements, it is called an *infinite set*.

The *cardinality* of a finite set A, denoted by $\#(A)$, is the number of elements in A. Thus, if D denotes the set of days of the week, $\#(D) = 7$. A set of cardinality one is known as a *singleton set*.

For an infinite set, one useful property we would like is some technique for listing the elements, i.e. we would like a method for specifying a first element, a second element etc. For example, if N denotes the positive integers, an obvious listing is $1, 2, 3, 4, \ldots$ and thus we can safely talk about 'the ith positive integer'. It is not obvious (and, indeed, not true) that every infinite set can be so listed.

Having listed the elements of N, the next question is: can we list the elements of Z, the set of all integers? The answer is yes. We simply alternate between positive and negative integers in increasing order of absolute value. This gives us the listing:

$$0, +1, -1, +2, -2, +3, -3, \ldots$$

Any $z \in Z$ will eventually appear in this list.

A *pair* of positive integers will be written as (n_1, n_2) where $n_1 \in N$ and $n_2 \in N$. The set of all such pairs is denoted by $N \times N$ and can be listed using a tableau method as illustrated in Table 1.1.

Whenever we can find a technique for listing all the elements of a set then we can use the term 'the ith element of the set' and in such a case we call the set *countable*. Clearly any finite set is countable, but this is not true of every infinite set. An example of an uncountably infinite set is $[0, 1)$—the set of all real numbers ≥ 0 and < 1. The proof of this result is based on a technique called *Cantor's diagonalization*. Let us assume we had some

Table 1.1

listing of all these real numbers and seek a contradiction. If we represent the numbers in the usual decimal notation then if our listing exists we can write

　　　1st real　　$0 \cdot a_{11} a_{12} a_{13} \ldots$

　　　2nd real　　$0 \cdot a_{21} a_{22} a_{23} \ldots$

　　　3rd real　　$0 \cdot a_{31} a_{32} a_{33} \ldots$

　　　　　　　　　. . .

　　　　　　　　　. . .

where each a_{ij} is a simple digit. Every real number $\in [0, 1)$ must eventually occur in this listing. Now, consider the real number

$$0 \cdot a_{11} a_{22} a_{33} \ldots$$

made up of the 'diagonal' entries. Change each a_{ii} to b_{ii} where

$$b_{ii} = \begin{cases} a_{ii} + 1 & \text{if } a_{ii} < 9, \\ 0 & \text{if } a_{ii} = 9. \end{cases}$$

Now, $0 \cdot b_{11} b_{22} b_{33} \ldots \in [0, 1)$ but does not occur in the list. This is because for any i, the ith digit of $0 \cdot b_{11} b_{22} b_{33} \ldots$ is b_{ii} and this differs from a_{ii}, the ith digit of the ith entry of our list. This contradiction shows that $[0, 1)$ cannot be countable.

PRODUCTS OF SETS

Let A_1, A_2 be two sets. Then the product, $A_1 \times A_2$, of A_1 and A_2 consists of all the pairs (a_1, a_2) where the first element, a_1, is in A_1 and the second element, a_2, is in A_2, i.e.

$$A_1 \times A_2 = \{(a_1, a_2) | a_1 \in A_1, a_2 \in A_2\}.$$

As a simple example, if $A_1 = \{0, 1\}$ and $A_2 = \{x, y, z\}$, then $A_1 \times A_2 = \{(0, x), (0, y), (0, z), (1, x), (1, y), (1, z)\}$. We have also met the product $N \times N$ when we were discussing countability.

The definition is extended to $A_1 \times A_2 \times A_3$, the set of all triples (a_1, a_2, a_3), $a_1 \in A$, $a_2 \in A_2$, $a_3 \in A_3$ and similarly to $A_1 \times A_2 \times \ldots \times A_n$, the set of all n-tuples $(a_1, a_2, \ldots, a_n)$ where $a_i \in A_i$, $i = 1, 2, \ldots, n$.

It can be shown that for finite sets, $\#(A_1 \times A_2) = \#(A_1) \times \#(A_2)$ and, by using a tableau, that $A_1 \times A_2$ is countable iff A_1 and A_2 are countable. An inductive argument can then be used to show that for any $n > 1$, $\#(A_1 \times A_2 \times \cdots \times A_n) = \#(A_1) \times \#(A_2) \times \ldots \times \#(A_n)$ for finite sets and that $A_1 \times A_2 \times \cdots \times A_n$ is countable iff $A_1, A_2, \ldots, A_n$ are countable.

A *relation* R is simply any subset of $A_1 \times A_2$, where A_1 is called the *domain* of R and A_2 is called the *range* of R. We will often be concerned with relations where the domain and range are the same set, A, say. We then say

$R \subset A \times A$ is a relation *on A*. For example, if $A = \{0, 1, 2, 3\}$ then the set of ordered pairs

$$L = \{(0, 1), (0, 2), (0, 3), (1, 2), (1, 3), (2, 3)\}$$

would be the relation corresponding to our notion of 'strictly less than', while

$$E = \{(0, 0), (1, 1), (2, 2), (3, 3)\}$$

would be the relation 'is equal to'. We will adopt the usual notation and write aRb for $(a, b) \in R$ and $aR\!\!\!/b$ for $(a, b) \notin R$.

A relation R on A is said to be *reflexive* if

aRa for all $a \in A$.

Thus L above is not a reflexive relation on A since $(0, 0) \notin L$, but E is reflexive.

A *symmetric* relation satisfies.

aRb implies bRa.

L is not symmetric since $(0, 1) \in L$ but $(1, 0) \notin L$. However, E is symmetric.

A *transitive* relation R on A satisfies:

aRb and bRc implies aRc.

Both L and E are transitive relations.

If a relation R on A is reflexive, symmetric and transitive then it is called an *equivalence relation*. We have shown that E is an equivalence relation on $A = \{0, 1, 2, 3\}$ but there are others, for example,

$$V = \{(0, 0), (0, 2), (1, 1), (1, 3), (2, 2), (2, 0), (3, 1), (3, 3)\}.$$

If R is an equivalence relation on A and $a \in A$ then associated with a is the set of elements, $\bar{a}$, comprising all the elements related to a by R. Thus

$$\bar{a} = \{b \in A \mid aRb\}$$

Such a set is called an *equivalence class*.

For E, there are four distinct equivalence classes, $\bar{0} = \{0\}$, $\bar{1} = \{1\}$, $\bar{2} = \{2\}$ and $\bar{3} = \{3\}$. For V, we have only two distinct equivalence classes $\bar{0} = \bar{2} = \{0, 2\}$ and $\bar{1} = \bar{3} = \{1, 3\}$. This illustrates the following theorem.

Theorem 1.2

The equivalence classes defined by an equivalence relation R on a set A partition A into a number of disjoint, nonempty sets.

Proof Each $\bar{a}$ is nonempty since $a \in \bar{a}$ (aRa since R is reflexive). We have to show that if $\bar{a}, \bar{b}$ denote two equivalence classes then either $\bar{a} = \bar{b}$ or $\bar{a} \cap \bar{b} = \emptyset$. If $\bar{a} \cap \bar{b} \neq \emptyset$ then there exists $c \in \bar{a} \cap \bar{b}$, i.e. $c \in \bar{a}$ and $c \in \bar{b}$. So, aRc

and bRc. Now, R is symmetric so bRc implies cRb, and R is transitive so aRc and cRb implies aRb. Thus $b \in \bar{a}$. Now, for all $x \in \bar{b}$, bRx and since aRb and R is transitive, it follows that aRx, i.e. $x \in \bar{a}$. This shows $\bar{b} \subset \bar{a}$. A similar argument can be used to show $\bar{a} \subset \bar{b}$ and thus $\bar{a} = \bar{b}$.

As a further illustration of equivalence classes, let R denote the relation on the positive integers, N, where aRb iff $|a - b|$ is divisible by 5. In this case, there are five distinct equivalence classes each of which have an infinite number of elements.

$$\bar{1} = \bar{6} = \bar{11} = \cdots,$$
$$\bar{2} = \bar{7} = \bar{12} = \cdots,$$
$$\bar{3} = \bar{8} = \bar{13} = \cdots,$$
$$\bar{4} = \bar{9} = \bar{14} = \cdots,$$

and $\quad \bar{5} = \bar{10} = \bar{15} = \cdots.$

If R is an arbitrary relation on A then the *reflexive* (respectively, *symmetric, transitive*) *closure* of R is the smallest reflexive (respectively, symmetric, transitive) relation on A with R as a subset. For example, if

$$R = \{(0, 1), (1, 1), (1, 2)\}$$

is a relation on $\{0, 1, 2\}$, then its reflexive closure is

$$\{(0, 0), (0, 1), (1, 1), (1, 2), (2, 2)\},$$

its symmetric closure is

$$\{(0, 1), (1, 0), (1, 1), (1, 2), (2, 1)\}$$

and its transitive closure is

$$\{(0, 1), (0, 2), (1, 1), (1, 2)\}.$$

As a further example, the relation $<$ defined on all integers has reflexive closure, $\leq$, symmetric closure, $\neq$, and since it is already transitive, its transitive closure is the relation itself.

A function $f : A \to B$ can be viewed as the set of all pairs (a, b) where $a \in A$, $b \in B$ and $b = f(a)$. Thus a function $f : A \to B$ can be defined as a relation in $A \times B$ with the property that if $(a, b) \in f$ and $(a, c) \in f$ then $b = c$. This last restriction simply means that $f(a)$ must be unique. If f is not defined on all elements of A, it is called a *partial function* $A \to B$ otherwise it is called a *total function* $A \to B$. The total function $f : A \to B$ is *onto* if for each $b \in B$, there exists $a \in A$ such that $f(a) = b$, and f is *one–one* if it maps unique elements of A to unique elements of B, i.e. if $f(a_1) = f(a_2)$ implies $a_1 = a_2$. In Fig. 1.1 we illustrate various functions, representing $(a, b) \in f$ by joining $a \in A$ to $b \in B$ by a directed line.

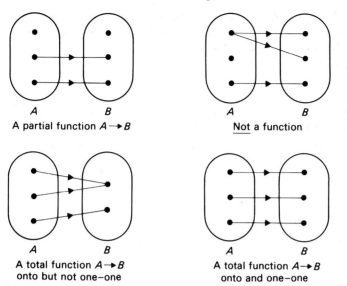

Figure 1.1

If a total function $f : A \to B$ is both onto and one–one we say that f is a *bijection*. We could define *countability* formally as follows: a set A is countable if it is either finite or there exists a bijection $f : A \to N$. This bijection specifies the listing of the elements where the ith element of A is mapped to the positive integer, i.

GRAPHS AND TREES

A *directed graph (digraph)*, $G = (V, E)$, consists of a finite set of *vertices* (or *nodes*), V, together with a relation E on V. We can represent a digraph diagrammatically as follows: for each $v \in V$, we draw the node $\textcircled{v}$ on the page and if $(v, w) \in E$ we join the node labelled v to the node labelled w by a directed line to get

Figure 1.2 gives the diagram representing the digraph $G_1 = (V_1, E_1)$ where $V_1 = \{v, w, x\}$ and $E_1 = \{(v, w), (v, x), (w, x), (x, v), (x, x)\}$.

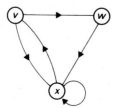

Figure 1.2

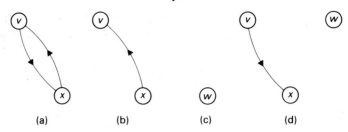

(a)   (b)   (c)   (d)

Figure 1.3

If, for some diagraph $G = (V, E), (v, w) \in E$ we say there is an *arc from v to w in G*. If there is a sequence of nodes $v = v_0, v_1, \ldots, v_n = w, n \geq 0$, such that $(v_i, v_{i+1}) \in E$ for $i = 0, 1, \ldots, n - 1$, then we say there is a *directed path from v to w in G of length n*. Thus the existence of a path from v to w implies that $v = w$ or we can get from the node labelled v to the node labelled w by following directed lines in our diagrammatic representation.

If $G = (V, E)$ is a diagraph then a (directed) subgraph of G is any digraph (V', E') where $V' \subset V$ and $E' \subset E$. Figure 1.3 illustrates four of the subgraphs of the digraph G_1 given in Fig. 1.2. Two subgraphs are said to be *disjoint* if they have no nodes in common. In Fig. 1.3, examples (a) and (c) and (b) and (c) are the only disjoint subgraphs.

An important type of digraph which we have already met in the introduction is a tree which can be defined recursively as follows. *A tree T = (V, E)* is a digraph where one node $r \in V$ is designated as the *root node*. If V contains just one node then $T = (\{r\}, \varnothing)$ otherwise T consists of the root, r, together with disjoint subgraphs $T_1, T_2, \ldots, T_k (k \geq 1)$ which are themselves trees and arcs from r to the roots of each of these trees. An example of a tree is given in Fig. 1.4. The reader should check that this conforms to our definition.

We can always draw trees with the root node at the top and arrows on the edges pointing downwards. Once this convention has been adopted the arrows are really superfluous and henceforth will be omitted.

A node in a tree which has no arcs going from it is variously called an *external node*, a *leaf node* or a *tip node*. Thus nodes labelled d, e, g, h and i are

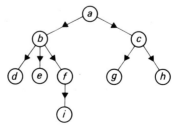

Figure 1.4

external nodes in Fig. 1.4. If a node is not an external node it is called an *internal node*. Much of the terminology concerned with trees is genealogical. For example, if there is an arc from a node v to a node w in a tree then we say v is the parent (node) of w. All nodes in a tree with the exception of the root have parent nodes. If v is a parent of w then we say w is a *child* of v and all internal nodes have children. If there is a directed path consisting of one or more arcs from a node v to a node w then v is said to be an *ancestor* of w and w a *descendant* of v.

STRINGS

Whenever we use the term *string* we mean a finite sequence of symbols $a_1 a_2 \ldots a_n$ where each a_i is taken from some finite alphabet Σ; repetitions are allowed. An example of a string of symbols from the alphabet $\Sigma = \{0, 1\}$ is 001110. If a string has m symbols counted according to multiplicity then we say the string has *length m*. Hence 001110 is a string of length 6. The *empty string*, denoted by ε, is a string of no symbols and has length 0. The length of a string, x, is denoted by $|x|$. Thus, $|001110| = 6$ and $|\varepsilon| = 0$.

The mathematics of strings is really very simple. We first must specify some *alphabet*. This is the nonempty, finite set of symbols which are going to appear in our strings. If the blank symbol occurs in the strings then it must be a member of the alphabet. To avoid confusion, the blank symbol is often represented in computing texts by $\wedge$; thus $00\wedge11\wedge01$ is written for 00 11 01. Notice that the blank symbol $\wedge$ is a string of length one—it must not be confused with the empty string.

Having specified the alphabet, Σ, we will denote the set of all finite length strings over the alphabet Σ by Σ^*. For example, if $\Sigma = \{0, 1\}$, then

$$\Sigma^* = \{\varepsilon, 0, 1, 00, 01, 10, 11, 000, 001, 010, \ldots\}.$$

Σ^* will always have a countably infinite number of elements (Exercise 1.3). Using normal set-theoretic notation, we write $x \in \Sigma^*$ if x is an element of Σ^* and $x \notin \Sigma^*$ if this is not the case. From the definition, it follows that $\varepsilon \in \Sigma^*$ for all sets, Σ.

If $x \in \Sigma^*$ is a string of length m, we can write $x = a_1 a_2 \ldots a_m$ where $a_i \in \Sigma$, $1 \le i \le m$. Then if $x \in \Sigma^*$ is a string of length m and $y \in \Sigma^*$ is a string of length n, the *concatenation* of x and y, denoted by xy, is defined to be the string of length $m + n$ whose first m symbols comprise a string equal to x and whose last n symbols comprise a string equal to y. Thus if $x = a_1 a_2 \ldots a_m$ and $y = b_1 b_2 \ldots b_n$ then $xy = a_1 a_2 \ldots a_m b_1 b_2 \ldots b_n$. Note that concatenation is an associative operation, i.e. $(xy)z = x(yz)$ but is obviously not commutative since, in general, $xy \ne yx$. The empty string acts as an identity with respect to concatenation since $\varepsilon x = x \varepsilon = x$ for all $x \in \Sigma^*$.

If a string $z \in \Sigma^*$ is of the form xy where $x, y \in \Sigma^*$ then x is said to be a *prefix* of z and y is said to a *postfix* of z. For example, if $z = 00110$ then according to the definition, ε is a prefix of z and so is $0, 00, 001, 0011$ and z itself. The postfixes of z are $\varepsilon, 0, 10, 110, 0110$ and z itself.

If $x, z \in \Sigma^*$ are such that $z = wxy$ for some $w, y \in \Sigma^*$ then x is said to be a *substring* of z. Thus, the substrings of $z = 00110$ are $\varepsilon, 0, 1, 00, 01, 10, 11, 001,$ $011, 110, 0011, 0110$ and z itself.

A (*formal*) *language L* over an alphabet Σ is simply defined as any subset of Σ^*. If L_1, L_2 are two such languages then their (*set*) *concatenation* is the language $L_1 L_2 = \{xy \mid x \in L_1, y \in L_2\}$. For example, if $L_1 = \{01, 0\}$ and $L_2 = \{\varepsilon, 0, 10\}$ then $L_1 L_2 = \{01, 0, 010, 00, 0110\}$. As with concatenation, set concatenation is associative but not commutative. For any language $L, L\{\varepsilon\} = \{\varepsilon\}L = L$ and thus the singleton set $\{\varepsilon\}$ acts as an identity for set concatenation. The singleton set containing the empty string is very different from the empty set, $\varnothing$, which acts as a zero for set concatenation since $L\varnothing = \varnothing L = \varnothing$ for any language, L.

If a language L is concatenated with itself the result LL is written as L^2. This definition is generalized to $L^0 = \{\varepsilon\}$, $L^1 = L$ and $L^i = LL^{i-1} = L^{i-1}L$ for $i \geq 2$. The *Kleene closure* of L, written L^*, is then defined as

$$\bigcup_{i=0}^{\infty} L^i.$$

L^+ is defined to be

$$\bigcup_{i=1}^{\infty} L^i$$

and hence, $L^* = L^+ \cup \{\varepsilon\}$. In particular, Σ^2 denotes all the strings in Σ^* of length two, Σ^3 denotes those of length three, etc. The set of strings over Σ of length greater than or equal to one is denoted by Σ^+ and hence

$$\Sigma^+ = \bigcup_{i=1}^{\infty} \Sigma^i$$

and

$$\Sigma^* = \Sigma^+ \cup \{\varepsilon\} = \bigcup_{i=0}^{\infty} \Sigma^i.$$

EXERCISES

1   If $A = \{ab, c\}$ and $B = \{c, ca\}$ are two languages in $\{a, b, c\}^*$, evaluate
   (a) $A \cup B$,
   (b) $A \backslash B$,
   (c) $A' \backslash B'$,
   (d) AB,
   (e) BA,
   (f) $A^2 \cup B^2$.

2 Show that the set of all rational numbers is countably infinite.

3 Show that if Σ is a finite alphabet then Σ^* is countably infinite.

4 The *depth of a node*, v, *in a tree*, $T = (V, E)$ is defined as follows: if v is the root node then the depth of v in T is 0; otherwise $v \in T_i$ for some subtree whose root is connected to the root of T by a single arc, and then the depth of v in T is one greater than the depth of v in T_i.

(a) Write down the depths of all the nodes in the tree given in Fig. 1.4. The *depth of a tree* is the greatest depth of any node in the tree.

(b) If T is a tree of depth k where every internal node has two children, show that T has n nodes where

$$2k + 1 \leq n \leq 2^{k+1} - 1.$$

5 Let T denote a tree. Show that there is a *unique* path from the root of T to any other node in the tree. (Hint: use an induction argument).

6 If $x \in \Sigma^*$ then the *reversal* of x, x^r, is defined recursively as follows: if $x = \varepsilon$ then $x^r = \varepsilon$; otherwise $x = ay$ where $a \in \Sigma$ and $y \in \Sigma^*$ and then $x^r = y^r a$. Write down a recursive definition for $|x|$, the length of a string $x \in \Sigma^*$ and use an induction argument to show that $|x| = |x^r|$, for all $x \in \Sigma^*$. (Hint: you may need to prove the result, $|xy| = |x| + |y|$, for all $x, y \in \Sigma^*$.)

7 Show that if R_1, R_2 are two relations on A then

(a) R_1 is reflexive implies $R_1 \cup R_2$ is reflexive;

(b) R_1 and R_2 are reflexive implies $R_1 \cap R_2$ is reflexive.

(c) Do these results remain true if every occurrence of 'reflexive' is replaced by 'symmetric'? What about replacing them by 'transitive'?

8 Let R be a relation in $A \times B$ and S a relation in $B \times C$. The *composition of R with S*, $R_0 S$, is defined to be the relation in $A \times C$ such that

$$R_0 S = \{(a, c) \mid \text{there exists } b \in B \text{ such that } (a, b) \in R \text{ and } (b, c) \in S\}.$$

(a) Show that composition is an associative operation.

(b) If R and S are total functions which are both onto, show that $R_0 S$ is also a total function A onto C.

9 If $R \subset A \times B$ is a relation then its *inverse*, R^{-1}, is a relation in $B \times A$ defined by

$$R^{-1} = \{(b, a) \mid (a, b) \in R\}.$$

(a) Show that $(R^{-1})^{-1} = R$.

(b) What conditions must be imposed on R if R^{-1} is a total function? If $A = B$ so that R is a relation on A, show

(c) R is reflexive iff R^{-1} is reflexive;

(d) R is symmetric iff R^{-1} is symmetric;

(e) R is transitive iff R^{-1} is transitive.

10   The set of all subsets of a set A is denoted by 2^A and is called the *power set* of A.

(a) If $A = \{a, b, c\}$ write out the eight elements in 2^A.

(b) Show that if $\#(A) = n$ then $\#(2^A) = 2^n$.

11   A function $f: 2^A \times 2^A \to 2^A$ is *monotonic increasing* if $A_1 \subset B_1$ and $A_2 \subset B_2$ implies $f(A_1, A_2) \subset f(B_1, B_2)$. Show that union and set concatenation are both monotonic increasing functions.

12   Let $G = (V, E)$ be a digraph and let E^* be the reflexive closure of the transitive closure of E. Show that there is a directed path from v to w in G, $v, w \in V$, iff $(v, w) \in E^*$.

Chapter 2

An Introduction to Grammars

Finite things reveal infinitude.

THEODORE ROETHKE
The Far Field

In most texts on a modern high-level programming language you will find a section devoted to the formal definition of the syntax. That of Pascal, for example, is usually given in the form of a number of *syntax charts*. Let us look closely at one of these syntax charts—the one defining the concept of 'factor' as given in Fig. 2.1.

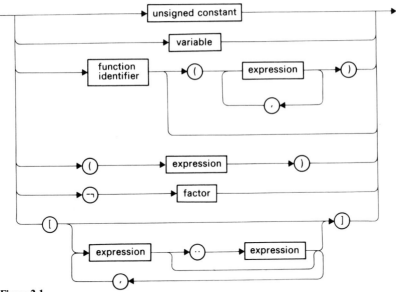

Figure 2.1

Any route through the syntax chart will pass through a number of nodes. For example, one simple route is

and this goes via just one node. A more complicated route via four nodes is

15

and even more complicated is

In fact, you should be able to see that there are an infinite number of possible routes through the syntax chart. Each route corresponds to a possible definition of factor. The syntax chart is a particularly neat way of giving these definitions. If you try and write out the definition of factor in English you will see how cumbersome it is.

Every node in the syntax chart which occurs in a square box, e.g. variable , is defined by some other chart. So, if a factor is defined to be a variable you will need to look up the definition of variable. These square nodes are *nonterminals*. If a node is encircled, e.g. Ⓞ, it is a *terminal* node and the contents of that node is a symbol of the language.

An alternative way of defining the syntax of Pascal would be to use BNF notation as used in the introduction of this book. In BNF notation, a nonterminal is surrounded by ⟨...⟩, the symbol :: = is used for 'is defined as' and | is used for 'or'. Our example definition of factor could then be written as follows

$$⟨ factor ⟩ :: = ⟨ unsigned constant ⟩$$
$$| ⟨ variable ⟩$$
$$| ⟨ function identifier ⟩$$
$$| ⟨ function identifier ⟩ (⟨ expression list ⟩)$$
$$| (⟨ expression ⟩)$$
$$| ¬⟨ factor ⟩$$
$$| [\quad]$$
$$| [⟨ two expression list ⟩]$$

where ⟨ expression list ⟩ and ⟨ two expression list ⟩ are new nonterminals defined by

$$⟨ expression list ⟩ :: = ⟨ expression ⟩$$
$$| ⟨ expression ⟩, ⟨ expression list ⟩$$

and

$$⟨ two expression list ⟩ :: = ⟨ two expression ⟩$$
$$| ⟨ two expression ⟩, ⟨ two expression list ⟩$$

where

$$⟨ two expression ⟩ :: = ⟨ expression ⟩$$
$$| ⟨ expression ⟩ ·· ⟨ expression ⟩$$

The use of syntax charts or BNF notation is completely interchangeable when defining programming languages. In '*PASCAL: User Manual and Report*', by K. Jensen and N. Wirth, published by Springer, you will find both the syntax chart definition and the BNF definition for the whole of the PASCAL syntax. Any valid program can be derived from the concept ⟨program⟩ using these rules. However, it should be noted that these syntax rules are not the whole story. There are additional constraints imposed on PASCAL programs that are not covered in these definitions—for example, the rule that every variable used in a program must appear in a declaration. This rule cannot be expressed using BNF notation or any equivalent notation. One main interest in formal language theory is to understand both the power and the limitations of BNF-like notation.

PHRASE STRUCTURE GRAMMARS

The formal model of a grammar which we will be defining is very similar to the BNF notation. In our formal model, we will use capital letters for nonterminals, lower case letters for terminals and replace $::=$ by $\rightarrow$. Thus a simple example grammar might look like

$$S \rightarrow A \mid B$$
$$A \rightarrow aA \mid a$$
$$B \rightarrow bB \mid b$$

From S we can derive either A or B. If we derive A then we can derive from A in one step the string a, or in two steps the string aa (by deriving aA from A and then expanding A as a) or in k steps a string of k a's, which we will denote by a^k. Similarly we can derive from B any string b^k for $k \geq 1$ in k steps.

If a string β can be derived from a string α by applying one of the derivation rules of the grammar, we write $\alpha \Rightarrow \beta$. If $\alpha_1 \Rightarrow \alpha_2$, $\alpha_2 \Rightarrow \alpha_3, \ldots, \alpha_{n-1} \Rightarrow \alpha_n (n \geq 1)$ we abbreviate this to $\alpha_1 \Rightarrow \alpha_2 \Rightarrow \cdots \Rightarrow \alpha_n$ or even more briefly as $\alpha_1 \overset{*}{\Rightarrow} \alpha_n$. Thus, using the above grammar,

$$S \Rightarrow A \Rightarrow aA \Rightarrow aaA \Rightarrow aaa$$

is a valid derivation of a^3 from S. We can also represent this derivation using a tree as in Fig. 2.2.

We now need to formalize these concepts. In the definition below, we generalize the derivation rules (which correspond to the formal notion of productions) to allow strings of terminals or nonterminals on the left-hand side as well as on the right-hand side. Up to now, all our examples have had just one nonterminal on the left-hand side and, indeed, such examples are the most important in computer science.

Chapter 2

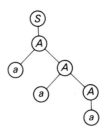

Figure 2.2

A *phrase structure grammar* (PSG) is a 4-tuple (N, T, P, S) where (a) N is a finite set of *nonterminals*. Conventionally elements of N are represented by upper-case letters (possibly subscripted); (b) T is a finite set of *terminals* such that $N \cap T = \emptyset$. Conventionally, the elements of T are represented by lower case letters (possibly subscripted and usually towards the beginning of the alphabet); (c) P is a finite set of *productions* of the form $\alpha \rightarrow \beta$ where α, the string on the left-hand side of the production, is such that $\alpha \in (N \cup T)^+$ and β, the string on the right-hand side of the production, is such that $\beta \in (N \cup T)^*$; (d) $S \in N$ is a symbol designated as the *start symbol* of the grammar.

An example PSG, G_1, is $(\{S, A, B\}, \{a, b\}, P, S)$ where P consists of productions

$$S \rightarrow A \quad S \rightarrow B$$
$$A \rightarrow aA \quad A \rightarrow a$$
$$B \rightarrow bB \quad B \rightarrow b$$

We will abbreviate the productions in a PSG using | for 'or' as usual. Thus the above productions are written

$$S \rightarrow A \,|\, B$$
$$A \rightarrow aA \,|\, a$$
$$B \rightarrow bB \,|\, b$$

As you may have noticed, once we have adopted our conventions of upper- and lower-case letters for nonterminals and terminals, it is only necessary to specify the productions and the start symbol to specify the grammar. If, as is usual, the start symbol is S, we will not have to specify that either.

Now, consider the PSG, G_2, with productions

$$S \rightarrow aSBC \,|\, aBC$$
$$CB \rightarrow BC$$
$$aB \rightarrow ab$$
$$bB \rightarrow bb$$

$$bC \rightarrow bc$$

$$cC \rightarrow cc$$

This is the first example we have seen where the left-hand side of the productions are not all single nonterminals. It can be shown that we can derive from S any string of the form $a^n b^n c^n, n \geq 1$. For example,

$S \Rightarrow aSBC$

$\Rightarrow aaBCBC$	(using $S \rightarrow aBC$)
$\Rightarrow aabCBC$	(using $aB \rightarrow ab$)
$\Rightarrow aabBCC$	(using $CB \rightarrow BC$)
$\Rightarrow aabbCC$	(using $bB \rightarrow bb$)
$\Rightarrow aabbcC$	(using $bC \rightarrow bc$)
$\Rightarrow aabbcc$	(using $cC \rightarrow cc$),

is a valid derivation of $a^2 b^2 c^2$.

By now you should have a good intuitive notion of what is meant by a 'derivation'. We will now use our formal definition of a grammar to state precisely what it means for a string to be derivable in a grammar. Let $G = (N, T, P, S)$ be any PSG and let $\gamma_1 \alpha \gamma_2 \in (N \cup T)^+$ be a string of terminals and nonterminals of length ≥ 1. If $\alpha \rightarrow \beta$ is a production in P then α in $\gamma_1 \alpha \gamma_2$ can be replaced by β to yield $\gamma_1 \beta \gamma_2$. In that case we write

$$\gamma_1 \alpha \gamma_2 \underset{G}{\Rightarrow} \gamma_1 \beta \gamma_2,$$

(read: $\gamma_1 \alpha \gamma_2$ generates $\gamma_1 \beta \gamma_2$ or $\gamma_1 \beta \gamma_2$ is derived from $\gamma_1 \alpha \gamma_2$).

If $\alpha_1, \alpha_2, \dots, \alpha_n \in (N \cup T)^*$ and $\alpha_1 \underset{G}{\Rightarrow} \alpha_2, \alpha_2 \underset{G}{\Rightarrow} \alpha_3, \dots, \alpha_{n-1} \underset{G}{\Rightarrow} \alpha_n \ (n > 1)$, we write

$$\alpha_1 \underset{G}{\Rightarrow} \alpha_2 \underset{G}{\Rightarrow} \alpha_3 \cdots \underset{G}{\Rightarrow} \alpha_{n-1} \underset{G}{\Rightarrow} \alpha_n$$

or in a more abbreviated form,

$$\alpha_1 \overset{+}{\underset{G}{\Rightarrow}} \alpha_n$$

(read: α_1 generates α_n in one or more steps). Thus $\overset{+}{\underset{G}{\Rightarrow}}$ is the transitive closure of the relation $\underset{G}{\Rightarrow}$. The reflexive closure of $\overset{+}{\underset{G}{\Rightarrow}}$ is denoted by $\overset{*}{\underset{G}{\Rightarrow}}$ and thus

$$\alpha_1 \overset{*}{\underset{G}{\Rightarrow}} \alpha_n \quad \text{iff} \quad \alpha_1 = \alpha_n \quad \text{or} \quad \alpha_1 \overset{+}{\underset{G}{\Rightarrow}} \alpha_n.$$

If $\alpha \in (N \cup T)^*$ is such that $S \overset{*}{\underset{G}{\Rightarrow}} \alpha$ then α is said to be a *sentential form of G*.

A *sentence* of G is then any sentential form in T^*, i.e. a terminal string which can be derived from S. The *language generated by* G, $L(G)$, is then defined to be the set of all sentences of G. Thus

$$L(G) = \{x \in T^* \mid S \overset{*}{\underset{G}{\Rightarrow}} x\}.$$

In many examples, the grammar G to which we are referring is clear from context. In such cases we can drop the subscript G from $\overset{+}{\underset{G}{\Rightarrow}}$, $\overset{*}{\underset{G}{\Rightarrow}}$ or $\overset{*}{\underset{G}{\Rightarrow}}$ and simply write $\Rightarrow$, $\overset{+}{\Rightarrow}$ or $\overset{*}{\Rightarrow}$.

Using the examples G_1, G_2 above, the reader should check that

$$L(G_1) = \{a^n \mid n \geq 1\} \cup \{b^n \mid n \geq 1\}$$

and

$$L(G_2) = \{a^n b^n c^n \mid n \geq 1\}.$$

Sometimes, it may be that two different grammars G and G' generate the same language $L(G) = L(G')$. In that case the grammars are said to be *equivalent*. An example of a grammar equivalent to G_1 is G_3 with productions

$$S \rightarrow aA \mid bB \mid a \mid b$$
$$A \rightarrow aA \mid a$$
$$B \rightarrow bB \mid b$$

CONTEXT-FREE GRAMMARS

The formal definition of the majority of the syntax of most programming languages can be defined using BNF notation. This corresponds to limiting the left-hand sides of each production $\alpha \rightarrow \beta$ in a PSG to be a single nonterminal. In formal language theory, PSGs with the productions so restricted are called *context-free grammars*. Formally, a context-free grammar (CFG) is a PSG, $G = (N, T, P, S)$ such that each production in P is of the form

$$A \rightarrow \beta \quad \text{where} \quad A \in N \quad \text{and} \quad \beta \in (N \cup T)^*.$$

Any language generated by a CFG is called a *context-free language* (CFL). The term context-free arises from the fact that any A in a sentential form can be expanded using a production of the form $A \rightarrow \beta$. It does not matter what strings surround A in the sentential form, the expansion is still valid.

G_1 is a CFG as is G_3. Hence $L = L(G_1) = L(G_3)$ is a CFL. At this stage, we cannot say whether $L_2 = L(G_2)$ is a CFL or not. Certainly, G_2 is not a context-free grammar but maybe there is some CFG which generates L_2. The reader may even like to try and construct such a CFG (but we will be

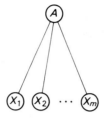

Figure 2.3

showing later that it would be a waste of time!). It is possible, however, to generate $\{a^n b^n \mid n \geq 1\}$ with a CFG, for example, by using the grammar with productions

$$S \rightarrow aSb \mid ab$$

Recall that if $G = (N, T, P, S)$ is a CFG then any $x \in L(G)$ can be derived from the start symbol, S. A convenient way of representing a derivation of a nonempty string x is by a *derivation tree* (sometimes called a *parse tree*). In such a tree, the root node is labelled S and the leaf nodes will be labelled, from left to right, $a_1, a_2, \ldots, a_n$ where $a_i \in T$, $1 \leq i \leq n$ and $x = a_1 a_2 \ldots a_n$. The internal nodes of the tree will be labelled with the nonterminal symbols used in the derivation of x. If A is such a symbol, which is expanded using the production $A \rightarrow X_1 X_2 \ldots X_m (X_i \in N \cup T, i = 1, \ldots, m)$, then the node labelled A is the parent of m nodes labelled $X_1, X_2, \ldots, X_m$ respectively, as illustrated in Fig. 2.3.

As an example, the derivation tree corresponding to the derivation of $a^3 b^2$ in the CFG, G_4, with productions

$$S \rightarrow AB$$
$$A \rightarrow aA \mid a$$
$$B \rightarrow bB \mid b$$

is given in Fig. 2.4.

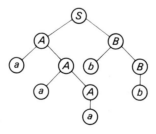

Figure 2.4

This derivation tree corresponds exactly with the derivation

$$S \Rightarrow AB$$
$$\Rightarrow aAB$$
$$\Rightarrow aaAB$$
$$\Rightarrow aaaB$$
$$\Rightarrow aaabB$$
$$\Rightarrow aaabb.$$

If $x \in L(G)$, then there will usually be many possible derivations of x. For example, in G_4, some alternative definitions of a^3b^2 are:

$$S \Rightarrow AB \Rightarrow AbB \Rightarrow aAbB \Rightarrow aaAbB \Rightarrow aaAbb \Rightarrow aaabb,$$
$$S \Rightarrow AB \Rightarrow aAB \Rightarrow aAbB \Rightarrow aAbb \Rightarrow aaAbb \Rightarrow aaabb,$$
and $S \Rightarrow AB \Rightarrow aAB \Rightarrow aaAB \Rightarrow aaAbB \Rightarrow aaabB \Rightarrow aaabb.$

Each of these will lead to identical derivation trees.

If, for all $x \in L(G)$, any derivation of x yields the same derivation tree, the CFG, G, is said to be *unambiguous*. If on the other hand, two or more distinct derivation trees exist for some $x \in L(G)$, G is said to be *ambiguous*. G_4 is an example of an unambiguous grammar.

A derivation of $x \in L(G)$ is said to be a *leftmost derivation* if it is always the leftmost nonterminal in the sentential form that is expanded. Since for any derivation tree there corresponds a unique leftmost derivation, we could redefine an ambiguous grammar to be any CFG such that there exists $x \in L(G)$ with two distinct leftmost derivations. One such ambiguous grammar is G_5 which has productions

$$S \rightarrow SbS \,|\, ScS \,|\, a$$

The string *abaca* is in $L(G_5)$ and it has two distinct leftmost derivations.

$$S \Rightarrow SbS \Rightarrow abS \Rightarrow abScS \Rightarrow abacS \Rightarrow abaca,$$
$$S \Rightarrow ScS \Rightarrow SbScS \Rightarrow abScS \Rightarrow abacS \Rightarrow abaca.$$

The derivation tree corresponding to the first derivation is given in Fig. 2.5a and that for the second in Fig. 2.5b.

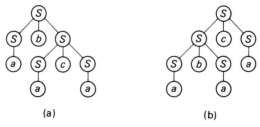

(a)   (b)

Figure 2.5

PARSING ARITHMETIC EXPRESSIONS

Consider the following simple BNF grammar designed to generate arithmetic expressions over the variables a,b,c.

$$\langle\,\text{expression}\,\rangle::=\quad\langle\,\text{term}\,\rangle|\langle\,\text{expression}\,\rangle+\langle\,\text{term}\,\rangle|\langle\,\text{expression}\,\rangle-\langle\,\text{term}\,\rangle$$
$$\langle\,\text{term}\,\rangle::=\quad\langle\,\text{factor}\,\rangle|\langle\,\text{term}\,\rangle\times\langle\,\text{factor}\,\rangle\quad\;|\langle\,\text{term}\,\rangle\,/\,\langle\,\text{factor}\,\rangle$$
$$\langle\,\text{factor}\,\rangle::=a|b|c|(\langle\,\text{expression}\,\rangle)$$

Using the formal notation of CFGs and setting E as our start symbol, we would write

$$E\rightarrow T|E+T|E-T$$
$$T\rightarrow F|T\times F|T\,/\,F$$
$$F\rightarrow a|b|c|(E)$$

This grammar is unambiguous since there exists a unique derivation tree for any string it generates. For example, the unique derivation tree for $a\times b+c$ is given in Fig. 2.6a. From this derivation tree, a compiler could construct another tree known as the *semantic tree*. The semantic tree for $a\times b+c$ is given in Fig. 2.6b and the reader should easily be able to see how it is constructed from the corresponding derivation tree. From the semantic tree, the compiler then constructs machine code equivalent to the original expression. Typical code for this example would be of the form

    LOAD a
    MULT b
    ADD c

The grammar we are using is a simplification of that used in the syntactic definition of PASCAL arithmetic expressions. Not only is the grammar unambiguous but also the productions have been cunningly arranged so that any semantic tree constructed from a derivation tree leads to the usual semantic interpretation. In particular, the standard priority of operators

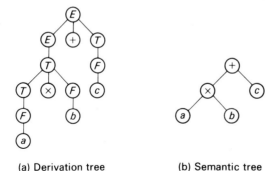

(a) Derivation tree   (b) Semantic tree

Figure 2.6

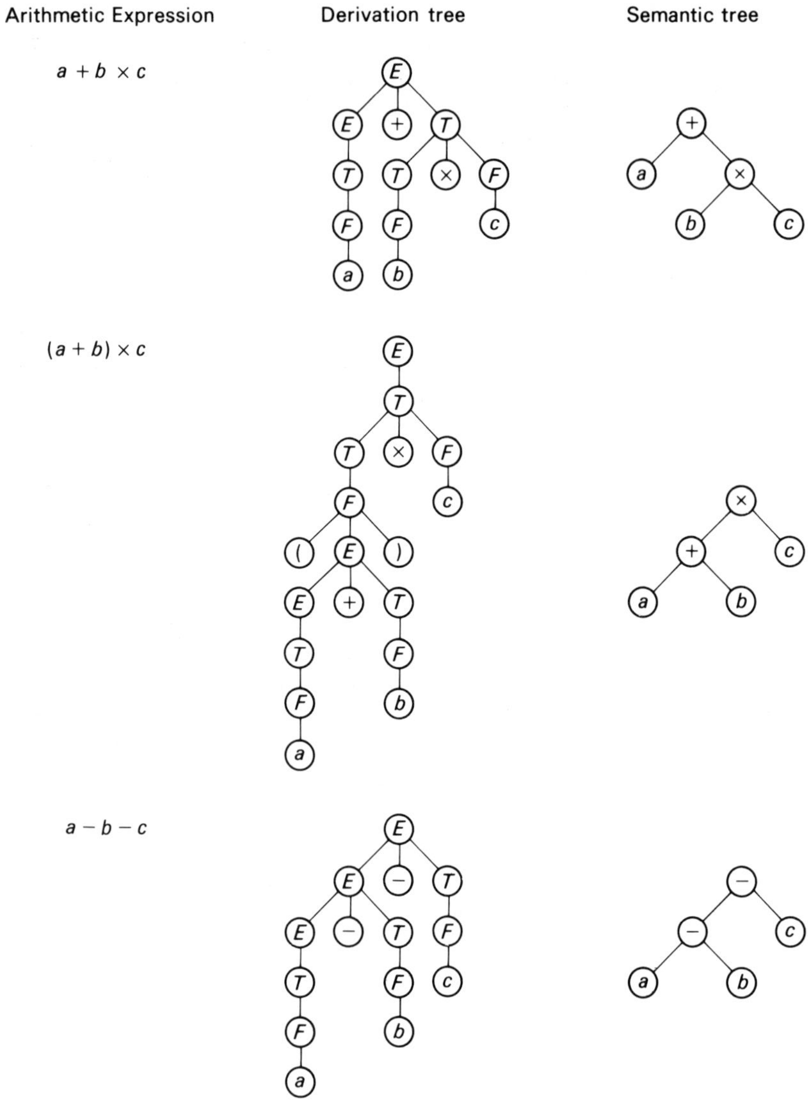

Arithmetic Expression	Derivation tree	Semantic tree
$a + b \times c$		

| $(a + b) \times c$ | | |

| $a - b - c$ | | |

Figure 2.7

($\times$ and $/$ first, then $+$ and $-$) is incorporated. Figure 2.7 gives some more illustrative examples.

It would be ideal if all the syntax of any programming language could be defined using CFGs. Much work has been done on these grammars and the techniques for constructing derivation trees are well understood. If the CFG has certain additional properties, which we will discuss in later chapters, efficient parsing algorithms can be designed. Unfortunately, although much of the syntax of a programming language can usually be defined in this way, there are always additional rules of the language which cannot be so expressed. Thus although the core of a compiler is the implementation of a parsing algorithm leading to the construction of an internal form such as a semantic tree, there are always other checks to be made, tables to be updated, etc.

THE EMPTY STRING IN CFG'S

In our definition of CFGs, the productions were constrained to be of the form $A \to \beta$ where A is a nonterminal and β is any string of nonterminals and terminals. This means that we are allowing productions of the form $A \to \varepsilon$. We will call such productions *ε-productions*. These productions can cause difficulties both in parsing and in the construction of formal proofs concerning grammars. In fact, if the reader was really on his guard, he would have already wondered how such productions were represented in derivation trees.[1] A grammar with no ε-productions is called *ε-free*. Ideally we would like all our CFGs to be ε-free but it is clear that if $\varepsilon \in L(G)$ for some CFG, G, then it is impossible to remove all the ε-productions from G without changing the language generated. Thus, the best that we can hope to do is to construct a CFG, G', from G such that G' is ε-free and $L(G') = L(G) \backslash \{\varepsilon\}$. Luckily, the construction is possible and not too difficult.

Let $G = (N, T, P, S)$ be any CFG with ε-productions. Then $G' = (N, T, P', S)$ where P' is constructed from P as follows:

1 Put all the ε-free productions of P into P'.

2 Find all the nonterminals $A \in N$ such that $A \overset{*}{\underset{G}{\Rightarrow}} \varepsilon$. We call such non-terminals *ε-generating*. Then, for each production $p \in P$ with one or more ε-generating nonterminals appearing in the right hand side, add to P any ε-free production which can be constructed from p by omitting one or more of these ε-generating nonterminals.

We will prove $L(G') = L(G) \backslash \{\varepsilon\}$. Firstly, however, we will give an example to illustrate the construction.

Let G have productions

$$S \to [E] \mid E$$
$$E \to T \mid E + T \mid E - T$$
$$T \to F \mid T \times F \mid T / F$$
$$F \to a \mid b \mid c \mid \varepsilon$$

then $S \overset{*}{\Rightarrow} \varepsilon$, $E \overset{*}{\Rightarrow} \varepsilon$, $T \overset{*}{\Rightarrow} \varepsilon$ and $F \overset{*}{\Rightarrow} \varepsilon$. Thus the ε-free grammar constructed

---

[1] We simply allow ⓔ as an external node.

from G has productions

$$S \to [E] | [\ ] | E$$
$$E \to T | E + T | E - T | E + | E - | + T | - T | + | -$$
$$T \to F | T \times F | T / F | T \times | T / | \times F | / F | \times | /$$
$$F \to a | b | c$$

Now, for the proof. We will first prove

Lemma   For all $A \in N$ and $x \in T^+$, $A \underset{G}{\overset{*}{\Rightarrow}} x$ iff $A \underset{G'}{\overset{*}{\Rightarrow}} x$.

Proof   There are two parts to this proof.

Firstly, to show $A \underset{G'}{\overset{*}{\Rightarrow}} x$ implies $A \underset{G}{\overset{*}{\Rightarrow}} x$ is straightforward since if $X \to \beta$ is a production in G' then $X \underset{G}{\overset{*}{\Rightarrow}} \beta$ can be shown quite simply. Thus any derivation of G' can also be achieved in G. To show that $A \underset{G}{\overset{*}{\Rightarrow}} x$ implies $A \underset{G'}{\overset{*}{\Rightarrow}} x$ for all $A \in N$ and $x \in T^+$ we proceed by induction on n, the number of steps in the derivation of x from A in G. If $n = 0$, the result is trivial. If $n = 1$, then there is a production $A \to x$ in G and since $x \neq \varepsilon$, this is also a production in G'. Hence $A \underset{G'}{\Rightarrow} x$. Now, assume the result holds for all derivations of a nonempty terminal string from a nonterminal in $\leq k$ steps. Say $A \underset{G}{\overset{*}{\Rightarrow}} x$ requires $k + 1$ steps. Then there is a production in P of the form $A \to X_1 X_2 \dots X_m$, $X_i \in N \cup T$, where $A \underset{G}{\Rightarrow} X_1 X_2 \dots X_m \underset{G}{\overset{*}{\Rightarrow}} x$. The terminal string x can be divided into substrings $x = x_1 x_2 \dots x_m$ such that if $X_i \in N$ then $X_i \underset{G}{\overset{*}{\Rightarrow}} x_i$ and if $X_i \in T$ then $X_i = x_i$ (and hence, by definition $X_i \underset{G}{\overset{*}{\Rightarrow}} x_i$). Some of the $x_i (1 \leq i \leq m)$ may be empty since there are ε-productions in G. Say $1 \leq i1 < i2 < \dots < ir \leq m$ are such that $x_{i1}, x_{i2}, \dots, x_{ir}$ are the nonempty strings. Then $x = x_{i1} x_{i2} \dots x_{ir}$ and $X_{ij} \underset{G}{\overset{*}{\Rightarrow}} x_{ij}$, $j = 1, \dots, r$. Each such derivation must take $\leq k$ steps so we know by our inductive hypothesis that $X_{ij} \underset{G'}{\overset{*}{\Rightarrow}} x_{ij}$, $j = 1, \dots, r$. Since $A \to X_{i1} X_{i2} \dots X_{ir}$ is a production in G' we thus deduce $A \underset{G'}{\overset{*}{\Rightarrow}} x$ and the result holds for all derivations of $k + 1$ steps. The result thus holds for all derivations by induction and the lemma is proved.

An immediate corollary to the lemma is that for all $x \in T^+$, $S \underset{G}{\overset{*}{\Rightarrow}} x$ iff $S \underset{G'}{\overset{*}{\Rightarrow}} x$. Thus $x \in L(G) \backslash \{\varepsilon\}$ iff $x \in L(G')$. We have proved

Theorem 2.1

For any CFL, L, there exists an ε-free CFG, G, such that $L(G) = L \backslash \{\varepsilon\}$.

In future, if $\varepsilon \in L$ for some CFL, L, then we can insist that the only ε-production in a CFG, G, generating L is of the form $S \to \varepsilon$. We can also assume that in this case S does not appear on the right hand side of any other production. The reasoning for this is as follows. Let $G = (N, T, P, S)$ be an ε-free grammar generating $L \backslash \{\varepsilon\}$. Then let S' be a new nonterminal symbol and define $G' = (N \cup \{S'\}, T, P \cup \{S' \to \varepsilon | S\}, S')$. G' has all the desired properties and is such that $L(G') = L$.

EXERCISES

1 Define CFGs to generate the following languages:

(a) all strings in $\{0, 1\}^*$ where every 0 has a 1 immediately to the right;

(b) all strings in $\{0, 1\}^*$ which are palindromes, i.e., are the same as their reversal;

(c) all strings in $\{0, 1\}^*$ where there are twice as many 0's as 1's.

2 Consider the CFG with productions

$$S \to AB$$
$$A \to SA | BB | bB$$
$$B \to b | aA | \varepsilon$$

Design an equivalent grammar with only one ε-production, $S \to \varepsilon$.

3 Show that the grammar with productions

$$S \to bA | aB$$
$$A \to a | aS | bAA$$
$$B \to b | bS | aBB$$

generates the language in $\{a, b\}^*$ composed of strings with an equal number of a's and b's (Hint: use induction to show that for any sentential form the number of a's added to the number of A's equals the number of b's added to the number of B's).

4 Prove that $L(G_2) = \{a^n b^n c^n | n \geq 1\}$ where G_2 is the example PSG given in this chapter.

5 Show that the grammar given in Exercise 2.3 is ambiguous. By considering the grammar with productions

$$S \to aBS | aB | bAS | bA$$
$$A \to bAA | a$$
$$B \to aBB | b$$

show that there is an unambiguous grammar generating the same language. (This is not always the case. There are *inherently ambiguous context-free languages*, i.e. languages for which there are no unambiguous grammars.)

6 If every production in a grammar G which is not an ε-production is of the form $A \rightarrow aB$ or $A \rightarrow a$, A, $B \in N$, $a \in T$ then G is called a *regular grammar*. Show that if G is regular then the ε-free grammar G' constructed from G in the proof of Theorem 2.1 will also be regular.

7   Use the PASCAL syntax to check if the following are valid PASCAL programs.

(a)   *program* ex (output);
      begin
               if $1 + 1 = 2$ *then* write ('hooray')
      end

(b)   *program* ex2;
      begin
      write $(1 + 1)$
      end.

(c)   *program* copy (f1, f2);
      var f1, f2; *file of* char;
      begin reset (f1); rewrite (f2);

               while not eof (f1) *do*
                         begin f2↑ := f1 ; put (f2); get (f1);
                         end

      end.

8   Construct a program which is valid according to the PASCAL syntax definition but will not be accepted by a PASCAL compiler.

Chapter 3

Regular Languages I

The difficulty in life is the choice.

GEORGE MOORE
The Bending of the Bough

The definition of an unsigned integer can be given in BNF using the following rules.

$\langle$ digit sequence $\rangle ::= 0|1|2|3|4|5|6|7|8|9$

$|0\langle$ digit sequence $\rangle|1\langle$ digit sequence $\rangle|2\langle$ digit sequence $\rangle$

$|3\langle$ digit sequence $\rangle|4\langle$ digit sequence $\rangle|5\langle$ digit sequence $\rangle$

$|6\langle$ digit sequence $\rangle|7\langle$ digit sequence $\rangle|8\langle$ digit sequence $\rangle$

$|9\langle$ digit sequence $\rangle$

$\langle$ unsigned integer $\rangle ::= 0|1|2|3|4|5|6|7|8|9$

$|1\langle$ digit sequence $\rangle|2\langle$ digit sequence $\rangle|3\langle$ digit sequence $\rangle$

$|4\langle$ digit sequence $\rangle|5\langle$ digit sequence $\rangle|6\langle$ digit sequence $\rangle$

$|7\langle$ digit sequence $\rangle|8\langle$ digit sequence $\rangle|9\langle$ digit sequence $\rangle$

In this example, every right-hand side is either a simple terminal symbol or of the form a terminal followed by a nonterminal. In any programming language, all the basic symbols (integers, identifiers, operators, reserved words, punctuation symbols, etc.) can be defined using this sort of rule. Since much of the time spent in compiling is devoted to recognizing such basic symbols, there is good reason to study grammars with productions of this form. Such grammars are called regular grammars and the languages they define are called regular languages. In this chapter we will show that these languages can be very efficiently recognized and that the grammars have many desirable properties. Unfortunately, regular grammars are very limited and are incapable of describing even quite simple programming constructs. Their use in compiling is thus restricted to the recognition of the basic symbols used in a program—this stage of compiling is called *scanning* or *lexical analysis*. Once scanning is completed, more sophisticated techniques are required to parse the whole program. We will be discussing some of these methods in later chapters.

REGULAR GRAMMARS

A phrase structure grammar $G = (N, T, P, S)$ is called a *regular grammar* provided:

(i) if there exists an ε-production in G then it is of the form $S \to \varepsilon$ and then S does not appear as a substring of the right-hand side of any other production in P;

(ii) all other productions are of the form

$$A \to a \text{ where } A \in N, \ a \in T$$

or

$$A \to aB \text{ where } A, B \in N \text{ and } a \in T.$$

A language is called a *regular language* iff it is generated by some regular grammar. From the definition and the comment following Theorem 2.1, it is clear that L is regular iff $L \setminus \{\varepsilon\}$ is generated by an ε-free regular grammar.

The regular grammar, G_1, with productions

$$S \to aS \,|\, aB$$
$$B \to bB \,|\, b$$

generates the regular language $L(G_1) = \{a^m b^n \,|\, m, n \geq 1\}$. This particular example is ε-free since $\varepsilon \notin L(G_1)$. The regular language $L = L(G_1) \cup \{\varepsilon\}$ is generated by the regular grammar with productions

$$S \to \varepsilon \,|\, aS_1 \,|\, aB$$
$$S_1 \to aS_1 \,|\, aB$$
$$B \to bB \,|\, b$$

Since each production in a regular grammar replaces a nonterminal by a string containing at most one nonterminal, it follows that every sentential form is either in T^* or contains just one element of N. Moreover any nonterminal in a sentential form must be the rightmost symbol in that sentential form.

If we have an ε-free regular grammar $G = (N, T, P, S)$ generating L we can easily construct an ε-free regular grammar $G^+ = (N, T, P^+, S)$ generating L^+. The technique is to construct the productions in P^+ from P by simply adding productions of the form $A \to aS$ for each production of the form $A \to a$ in P. Thus G_1 would lead to G_1^+ with productions

$$S \to aS \,|\, aB$$
$$B \to bB \,|\, b \,|\, bS$$

Reverting back to the general case, we need to formally prove that $L(G^+) = L^+$, i.e. we need to prove $L(G^+) \subset L^+$ and that $L^+ \subset L(G^+)$.

$L(G^+) \subset L^+$ If $x \in L(G^+)$ then we show that $x \in L^+$ by induction on n, the number of 'new' productions (i.e. those in $P^+ \backslash P$) used in the derivation of x. If $n = 0$, then the derivation used just productions in P, so $x \in L$ and hence $x \in L^+$. Assume that if $n < k$ then $x \in L^+$ and consider a derivation of $x \in L(G^+)$ which uses k new productions. Let $A \to aS$ be the last such production. Then $S \overset{+}{\underset{G^+}{\Rightarrow}} yA \underset{G^+}{\Rightarrow} yaS \overset{+}{\underset{G^+}{\Rightarrow}} yaz = x$, where $y, z \in T^+$ and $a \in T$. Now, $yaS \overset{+}{\underset{G^+}{\Rightarrow}} yaz$ involves no new productions so $yaS \overset{+}{\underset{G}{\Rightarrow}} yaz$ and hence $S \overset{+}{\underset{G}{\Rightarrow}} z$, i.e. $z \in L$. Also, since $A \to aS$ is a new production, there must exist a production $A \to a$ in P. Hence $S \overset{+}{\underset{G^+}{\Rightarrow}} yA \underset{G}{\Rightarrow} ya$ is a derivation of $ya \in L(G^+)$ involving less than k new productions. Hence $ya \in L^+$ by the induction hypothesis. But, $ya \in L^+$ and $z \in L$ implies $x = yaz \in L^+$ and hence the result is proved.

$L^+ \subset L(G^+)$: If $x \in L^+$ then $x \in L^n$ for some $n \geq 1$. We will prove by induction on n that $x \in L^n$ implies $x \in L(G^+)$. If $n = 1$, $x \in L$ so x can be generated from S using just the productions in G. Since all these productions are also in P^+, this is a valid derivation in G^+ and hence $x \in L(G^+)$. Assume the result holds for all $n < k$ and consider $x \in L^k$. Thus $x = yz$ where $y \in L$ and $z \in L^{k-1}$. Let $S \overset{+}{\underset{G}{\Rightarrow}} y$ be a derivation of y in G. The last production used in this derivation is of the form $A \to a$ where $y = y'a$, $y' \in T^*$. Thus $A \to aS$ is a production in P^+ and hence yS is a sentential form of G^+. By the induction hypothesis there is a valid derivation of z from S in G^+ and hence $yz \in L(G^+)$. The result thus follows by induction.

Now, let L be any regular language then $L^* = (L \backslash \{\varepsilon\})^+ \cup \{\varepsilon\}$. We have shown that $(L \backslash \{\varepsilon\})^+$ is a regular language and hence so is L^*. We have thus proved the first part of the following result

Theorem 3.1

(a) If L is a regular language then so is L^*, the Kleene closure of L.
(b) If L_1, L_2 are regular languages then so are $L_1 \cup L_2$ and $L_1 L_2$.

The proof of the second part of this theorem also relies on constructing new grammars from old. We will describe the constructions here but leave the details of the proof to the reader.

Firstly, to prove the union result, we can assume L_1, L_2 do not contain ε. (If $\varepsilon \in L_1$ or $\varepsilon \in L_2$ then $\varepsilon \in L_1 \cup L_2$ and the grammar generating $L_1 \cup L_2$ can easily be constructed from one generating $(L_1 \backslash \{\varepsilon\}) \cup (L_2 \backslash \{\varepsilon\})$.) Before describing the construction let us first consider an example. Let $L_1 = \{a^m b^n | m, n \geq 1\}$ be the language generated by the grammar G_1 described above and let L_2 be that generated by G_2 with productions

$$S \to cS \mid c$$

Hence $L_2 = \{c^n \mid n \geq 1\}$. Our first attempt at a grammar which generates $L_1 \cup L_2$ might be to simply write down all the productions of G_1 and all the productions of G_2. This would be wrong since we could get the productions muddled in a derivation and generate strings $\notin L_1 \cup L_2$. In our example, we could get

$$S \Rightarrow aS \Rightarrow ac$$

We must make sure that any derivation uses either just productions of G_1 or just productions of G_2. To achieve this we need distinct nonterminal symbols for G_1 and G_2. So, we rewrite $G_1 = (\{S_1, B_1\}, \{a, b\}, P_1, S_1)$ with productions, P_1, defined by

$$S_1 \to aS_1 \mid aB_1$$
$$B_1 \to bB_1 \mid b$$

and $G_2 = (\{S_2\}, \{c\}, P_2, S_2)$ where P_2 is defined by

$$S_2 \to cS_2 \mid c$$

S_1, B_1 and S_2 are distinct symbols. We now want to combine all these productions and choose for our start symbol either S_1 or S_2. We can only have one start symbol so let us introduce a new symbol, S. We cannot write $S \to S_1 \mid S_2$ since such productions are not valid in regular grammars. What we can do instead is to have productions of the form $S \to \alpha$ for all α such that either $S_1 \to \alpha$ is a production in G_1 or $S_2 \to \alpha$ is one in G_2. The regular grammar constructed for our example thus has productions

$$S \to aS_1 \mid aB_1 \mid cS_2 \mid c$$
$$S_1 \to aS_1 \mid aB_1$$
$$B_1 \to bB_1 \mid b$$
$$S_2 \to cS_2 \mid c$$

It is not difficult to see that this grammar generates $\{a^m b^n \mid m, n \geq 1\} \cup \{c^n \mid n \geq 1\}$.

With the benefit of the above discussion, we can now write out the formal construction. Let $G_1 = (N_1, T_1, P_1, S_1)$ and $G_2 = (N_2, T_2, P_2, S_2)$ be ε-free regular grammars generating L_1 and L_2 respectively. Without loss of generality, we can assume $N_1 \cap N_2 = \emptyset$. Let $S \notin N_1 \cup N_2$ be a new symbol and construct $G = (N_1 \cup N_2 \cup \{S\}, T_1 \cup T_2, P_1 \cup P_2 \cup P_3, S)$ where P_3 is the set of all productions $S \to \alpha$ where $S_1 \to \alpha$ is in P_1 or $S_2 \to \alpha$ is in P_2. The reader should construct a formal proof that $L(G) = L(G_1) \cup L(G_2)$.

We can also construct another grammar, G' from G_1 and G_2 such that

$L(G') = L(G_1)L(G_2)$. Remembering $N_1 \cap N_2 = \emptyset$, $G' = (N_1 \cup N_2, T_1 \cup T_2, P', S_1)$ where P' is the set of all productions of P_1 and P_2 except that each production of P_1 of the form $A \to a$ is replaced by $A \to aS_2$. Again the reader is invited to construct a formal proof of the result. For our example, the construction yields

$$S_1 \to aS_1 \mid aB_1$$
$$B_1 \to bB_1 \mid bS_2$$
$$S_2 \to cS_2 \mid c$$

FINITE STATE AUTOMATA

Any regular grammar $G = (N, T, P, S)$ can be represented as a directed graph with labelled arcs and nodes. There are distinct nodes in the graph each labelled with an element of N as well as one specially designated 'halt' node labelled #. By convention, the node labelled with the start symbol, S, is highlighted by an arrow and the halt node by being in a square (as opposed to a circle). If there exists a production $A \to aB$ in P then the node labelled A is joined to the node labelled B with a directed arc labelled a. If there is a production $A \to a$ in P then the node labelled A is joined to the node labelled # by a directed arc labelled a. Each arc in the graph will thus correspond to precisely one production in P.

The regular grammar G_3 with productions

$$S \to aA \mid bB$$
$$A \to aA \mid a$$
$$B \to bB \mid b$$

is thus represented by the labelled digraph given in Fig. 3.1.

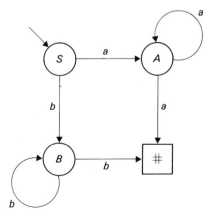

Figure 3.1

Now, trace out any path from the start node, labelled S, to the halt node (sometimes called the final node), labelled #. The labels associated with the arcs comprising your path will make up a string. The set of all such strings is precisely $L(G_3)$ and each path corresponds in a natural way to a derivation. Thus the path from ⑤ to ④, to ④ again, to ④ again and then to ⊞ corresponds to the derivation $S \Rightarrow aA \Rightarrow aaA \Rightarrow aaaA \Rightarrow aaaa$.

A labelled digraph with a designated start node and one (or more) final nodes describes a finite state automaton (sometimes known as a finite state machine). We will at first restrict our study to *deterministic* finite state automata where at most one arc with a given label leaves any node. The example given in Fig. 3.1 is nondeterministic since there are two arcs labelled a leaving the node labelled A.

A *deterministic finite state automaton* (DFSA) is a 5-tuple $M = (K, T, t, k_1, F)$ where

(a) K is a finite set of *states*,

(b) T is a finite *input alphabet*,

(c) t is a (possibly partial) *transition function* $K \times T \rightarrow K$ which given a state and an input delivers the next state to be visited,

(d) $k_1 \in K$ is a designated *start state*,

(e) $F \subset K$ is a set of *final states*. (Note: any state in K can be designated to be a final state.)

We will continue to represent a DFSA as a labelled digraph with the states represented as nodes and the convention that the start state, k_1, is arrowed and any final state $k \in F$ is denoted in a square (rather than in a circle). An example DFSA is illustrated in Fig. 3.2. Written as a 5-tuple this DFSA is $(\{A, B, C, D, E\}, \{a, b\}, t, A, \{D, E\})$ where the transition function, t,

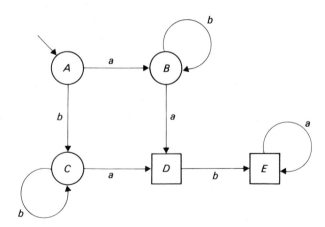

Figure 3.2

can be tabulated as follows:

state (K)	input (T)	next state (K)
A	a	B
A	b	C
B	a	D
B	b	B
C	a	D
C	b	C
D	b	E
E	a	E

Note that t is a partial function since $t(D, a)$ and $t(E, b)$ are both undefined. An alternative and neater representation for t is as a *transition array*. If $M = (K, T, t, k_1, F)$ is a DFSA then the transition array, A_t, representing t is a $\#(K) \times \#(T)$ integer matrix. If the states are ordered $k_1, k_2, \ldots, k_n$ and the alphabet is ordered $a_1, a_2, \ldots, a_m$ then $A_t(i, j) = l$ iff $t(k_i, a_j) = k_l$. If both the states and the input alphabet in our example are ordered alphabetically, the resulting transition array is

$$\begin{pmatrix} 2 & 3 \\ 4 & 2 \\ 4 & 3 \\ . & 5 \\ 5 & . \end{pmatrix}$$

If t is partial (as in this example) then not all the entries of A_t will be defined.

We are interested in the strings comprising labels on the paths from the start state of a DFSA to any of the final states. The set of all such strings for a given DFSA, M, is denoted by $T(M)$ and is called the *set of strings accepted by M*. To formally define this, we need to first extend t from a function $K \times T \to K$ to a function $K \times T^* \to K$. If $k \in K$ and $x \in T^*$ then we want $t(k, x)$ to denote the state we would reach if we were in the state labelled k and then followed a path labelled x. Clearly, if $x = \varepsilon$ then $t(k, \varepsilon) = k$. Otherwise $x = ay$ for some $a \in T$, $y \in T^*$ and we can then define t recursively by $t(k, x) = t(t(k, a), y)$.

Using our example,

$$t(A, aba) = t(t(A, a), ba)$$
$$= t(B, ba)$$
$$= t(t(B, b), a)$$
$$= t(B, a) = D.$$

The set of strings $T(M) \subset T^*$ which is accepted by a DFSA $M = (K, T, t, k_1, F)$ can now be defined:

$$T(M) = \{x \in T^* | t(k_1, x) \in F\}.$$

If the fact that the transition function, t, in a DFSA, M, may be partial is troubling you, then this can be remedied by observing that $T(M)$ will be unaffected if you add a new (dummy) state, Δ, and where previously $t(k, a)$ was undefined you now set $t(k, a) = \Delta$. Also, you will need to set $t(\Delta, a) = \Delta$ for all $a \in T$. If this construction is used on our example, the DFSA of Fig. 3.3 is constructed. (The arc from Δ with two labels a, b is just a standard shorthand notation for two arcs—one labelled a, the other labelled b.) What perhaps is more worrying is the restriction in the definition which makes the finite state automaton deterministic. The next step is to remedy this situation and allow more than one arc with a given label to leave a state. This means that when the transition function, t, is applied to an element of $K \times T$ it delivers a set of possible next states rather than a single next state. If there are no next states for a given pair $(k, a) \in K \times T$ then $t(k, a) = \varnothing$ and since $\varnothing \in 2^K$, $t: k \times T \rightarrow 2^K$ is always a total function.

A *nondeterministic finite state automaton* (NFSA) is a 5-tuple, $M = (K, T, t \; k_1, F)$, where

(a) K is a finite set of *states*,
(b) T is a finite *input alphabet*,
(c) t is a total function $K \times T \rightarrow 2^K$, called the *transition function*,
(d) $k_1 \in K$ is a designated *start state*,
(e) $F \subset K$ is a set of *final states*.

The finite state automaton given in Fig. 3.1 is nondeterministic and its

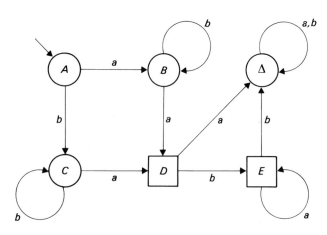

Figure 3.3

transition function can be tabulated as follows

K	T	2^K
S	a	$\{A\}$
S	b	$\{B\}$
A	a	$\{A, \#\}$
A	b	$\emptyset$
B	a	$\emptyset$
B	b	$\{B, \#\}$
$\#$	a	$\emptyset$
$\#$	b	$\emptyset$

Before defining the set of strings accepted by such a NFSA we again need to extend our transition function, t. Firstly, we extend it to operate on $2^K \times T$ by defining

$$t(K',a) = \bigcup_{k \in K'} t(k,a)$$

for $K' \subset K, a \in T$.

Thus, if the automaton is in any of the states in K' and we follow an arc labelled $a \in T$ then the set of states that we can possibly reach is precisely $t(K',a)$. We now extend t yet again but this time to be a function $2^K \times T^* \to 2^K$. We use the same technique that we used for DFSAs. If $K' \subset K$ then $t(K',\varepsilon) = K'$ and if $x = ay, a \in T, y \in T^*$, then $t(K',x) = t(t(K',a), y)$.

Using the NFSA given in Fig. 3.1, we have, for example,

$$
\begin{aligned}
t(\{S, A\}, ab) &= t(t(\{S, A\}, a), b) \\
&= t(t(S,a) \cup t(A,a), b) \\
&= t(\{A, \#\}, b) \\
&= t(A,b) \cup t(\#, b) = \emptyset.
\end{aligned}
$$

Now, for an arbitrary NFSA $M = (K, T, t, k_1, F)$ we define $T(M)$, the *set of strings accepted by M* to be exactly those strings which correspond to the labels on paths which can get you from a start state to a final state. Formally,

$$T(M) = \{x \in T^* \mid t(\{k_1\}, x) \cap F \neq \emptyset\}.$$

At first, it appears that NFSAs might be considerably more powerful than DFSAs but, surprisingly perhaps, this is not the case.

Theorem 3.2

L can be accepted by a DFSA iff L can be accepted by a NFSA.

Proof $\Rightarrow$: For any DFSA there exists an equivalent DFSA with a total transition function which can be easily constructed by adding a dummy state. We thus assume that $L \subset T^*$ is such that $L = T(M)$ for some DFSA $M = (K, T, t, k_1, F)$ where t is total. Such a DFSA can be made into a NFSA $M' = (K, T, t', k_1, F)$ simply be defining $t'(k, a) = \{t(k, a)\}$. It follows from the definitions that $T(M) = T(M')$.

$\Leftarrow$: Let $M = (K, T, t, k_1, F)$ be a NFSA then we will construct a DFSA which accepts $T(M)$. The DFSA will have a set of states equal to 2^K, i.e. all possible subsets of K, an input alphabet, T, a start state $\{k_1\}$ and a transition function defined to be the extension of t which acts on $2^K \times T \to 2^K$. Now, by definition, $x \in T(M)$ iff $t(\{k_1\}, x) \cap F \neq \emptyset$ so if we set the final states of the DFSA to be precisely those sets $K' \subset K$ such that $K' \cap F = \emptyset$ then the construction is completed.

In practice, it is a fairly straightforward task to take an example NFSA and construct an equivalent DFSA, i.e. one that accepts the same language. We can confine our attention to those states which can be reached from the start state, $\{k_1\}$. Thus, rather than construct all $2^{*(K)}$ possible states, we

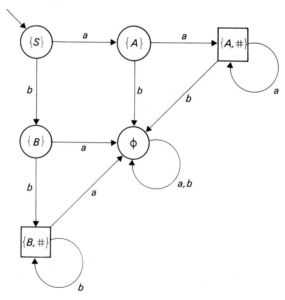

Figure 3.4

simply begin with $\{k_1\}$ and calculate $t(\{k_1\}, a)$ for all $a \in T$. This gives a number of new states to be connected to $\{k_1\}$. Then, for each state K' so created we again calculate $t(K', a)$ for all $a \in T$ and introduce new states if necessary. This process is repeated until no new states are created. Since the total number of states constructed is at worst $2^{\#(K)}$, the process is bound to terminate. The DFSA constructed in this way which is equivalent to the NFSA represented in Fig. 3.1 is represented in Fig. 3.4. You will notice that $\varnothing$ acts as a dummy state and, in fact, $\varnothing$ and all arcs to it could be omitted.

We are now in a position to prove the major result of this section on finite state automata.

Theorem 3.3

The following statements are equivalent:
 (i) L is accepted by a NFSA;
 (ii) L is accepted by a DFSA;
 (iii) L is generated by a regular grammar.

Proof We have already shown the equivalence of parts (i) and (ii) in Theorem 3.2. We will now give the constructions required to show (ii) $\Rightarrow$ (iii) and (iii) $\Rightarrow$ (i). The reader is left to complete the formal proofs.

(ii) $\Rightarrow$ (iii): Let L be accepted by the DFSA $M = (K, T, t, k_1, F)$. Without loss of generality, we can assume $K \cap T = \varnothing$. We will construct a regular grammar G such that $L(G) = T(M) \backslash \{\varepsilon\}$. [If $\varepsilon \in T(M)$ then $k_1 \in F$ and we can easily construct a regular grammar G' from G such that $L(G') = L(G) \cup \{\varepsilon\} = T(M)$]. The grammar we require is $G = (N, T, P, S)$ where $N = K$, $S = k_1$ and P consists of all productions $k_i \to ak_j$ where $t(k_i, a) = k_j$ together with all productions $k_i \to a$ where $t(k_i, a) = k_j$ and $k_j \in F$. For example, renaming the states of Fig. 3.4 and omitting the dummy state gives the DFSA of Fig. 3.5. This has an associated grammar with states $\{k_1, k_2, k_3, k_4, k_5\}$, start state, k_1, and productions

$$k_1 \to ak_2 \,|\, bk_4$$
$$k_2 \to ak_3 \,|\, a$$
$$k_3 \to ak_3 \,|\, a$$
$$k_4 \to bk_5 \,|\, b$$
$$k_5 \to bk_5 \,|\, b$$

The reader should formally prove that $x \in L(G)$ iff $x \in T(M) \backslash \{\varepsilon\}$.

(iii) $\Rightarrow$ (i): This is the construction that motivated our study of finite state automata in the first place. If $L = L(G)$ is generated by $G = (N, T, P, S)$ then L is accepted by a NFSA $= (N \cup \{\#\}, T, t, \{S\}, \{\#\})$ where $\#$ is a new symbol $\notin N$ and t is defined according to the following rules. If $A \to a$ is a production of P then $t(A, a)$ contains $\#$ and if $A \to aB$ is a production in P then $t(A, a)$

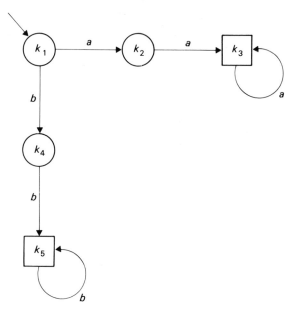

Figure 3.5

contains B. The only members of $t(A, a)$ are those obtained by applying these rules.

The fact that for any regular language L there is a DFSA, M, such that $T(M) = L$ gives us an efficient way to test whether an arbitrary string, x, is in L or not. We simply construct M and see if there is a path labelled x from the start state to a final state. By insisting that M is deterministic we know that there is at most one path labelled x which can be taken from the start state. If we wish, we may also use a dummy state and then we always have exactly one path from the start state for any $x \in T^*$ and all we need do is to check if it takes us to a final state.

Having shown that regular languages are precisely those languages accepted by DFSAs or NFSAs, we can use this powerful result to prove some interesting theorems.

Theorem 3.4

If L is a regular language in T^*, then so is the complement of $L, \bar{L} = T^* \backslash L$. *Proof*   Let $M = (K, T, t, k_1, F)$ be a DFSA accepting L. By the introduction of a dummy state (if necessary), we can insist that the transition function, t, is total. If $x \in L$ then in the digraph for M there is a path labelled x

from k_1 to a final state. If $x \notin L$ then the path from k_1 labelled x must lead to a nonfinal state. Thus $\bar{L}$ is accepted by $\bar{M} = (K, T, t, k_1, K \backslash F)$ and hence must a be regular language.

Theorem 3.5

If L_1, L_2 are regular languages then so is $L_1 \cap L_2$, the intersection of L_1, L_2. *Proof* $\bar{L}_1, \bar{L}_2$ are both regular languages by Theorem 3.4. Thus, by Theorem 3.1b so is $\bar{L}_1 \cup \bar{L}_2$. The result follows by applying Theorem 3.4 again since $L_1 \cap L_2 = \overline{\bar{L}_1 \cup \bar{L}_2}$.

FINITE STATE AUTOMATA WITH ε-MOVES

If the definition of a NFSA is altered so that moves from one state to another can be accomplished without necessitating any input we say that the automaton has ε-moves. More formally, a NFSA $M = (K, T, t, k_1, F)$ has ε-moves if t, instead of being a function $K \times T \to 2^K$, is defined as a function $K \times (T \cup \{\varepsilon\}) \to 2^K$. In Fig. 3.6, we give an example of such a NFSA.

If $M = (K, T, t, k_1, F)$ is an NFSA with ε-moves and $k, k' \in K$ are such that $k' \in t(k, \varepsilon)$, we then say k' is *ε-reachable* from k and write $k \underset{\varepsilon}{-} k'$. Thus, in such a case, the NFSA M can pass from state k to k' without reading any input. Let $\underset{\varepsilon}{\overset{*}{-}}$ be the reflexive, transitive closure of $\bar{\varepsilon}$. Then $k \underset{\varepsilon}{\overset{*}{-}} k'$ iff $k = k'$ or there exists a path from k to k' of length ≥ 1 with each arc labelled ε. If $k \in K$, then the set of states reachable from k without requiring further input is denoted by $R(k)$ so $R(k) = \{k' | k \underset{\varepsilon}{\overset{*}{-}} k'\}$. This definition is extended such

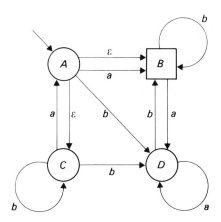

Figure 3.6

that if $K' \subset K$ then

$$R(K') = \bigcup_{k \in K'} R(k).$$

In the example, $R(A) = \{A, B, C\}$, $R(B) = \{B\}$, $R(C) = \{C\}$ and $R(D) = \{D\}$. Thus, $R(\{A, B\}) = R(A) \cup R(B) = \{A, B, C\}$, etc.

Our first task is to extend the transition function t of our NFSA with ε-moves to get a function $\hat{t}: K \times (T \cup \{\varepsilon\}) \to 2^K$ in such a way that if $k \in K$ then $\hat{t}(k, a)$ is the set of states that we can reach if we start in state k and have an input a. Because of the ε-moves, $\hat{t}$ is not simply t. For instance, if we are in state A in our example then $t(A, a) = \{B\}$ but you can also reach D, A itself and C with an input of just a. To reach D you first go to B using no input and then go to D using a; to reach A you go to C using no input and then return to A using input a. C can then also be reached without further input. We thus define $\hat{t}: K \times (T \cup \{\varepsilon\}) \to 2^K$ by

$$\hat{t}(k, \varepsilon) = R(k)$$

and

$$\hat{t}(k, a) = \bigcup_{k' \in R(k)} R(t(k', a)), \text{ for all } k \in K, a \in T.$$

In the example,

$$\hat{t}(A, \varepsilon) = R(A) = \{A, B, C\},$$

$$\hat{t}(A, a) = \bigcup_{k' \in \{A, B, C\}} R(t(k', a))$$
$$= R(\{B\}) \cup R(\{D\}) \cup R(\{A\})$$
$$= \{A, B, C, D\},$$

$$\hat{t}(A, b) = \bigcup_{k' \in \{A, B, C\}} R(t(k', b))$$
$$= R(\{D\}) \cup R(\{B\}) \cup R(\{C, D\})$$
$$= \{B, C, D\},$$

etc.

We now extend $\hat{t}$ to be a function $2^K \times (T \cup \{\varepsilon\}) \to 2^K$ in the obvious way by defining for $K' \subset K$ and $a \in T$

$$\hat{t}(K', \varepsilon) = R(K'),$$

and

$$\hat{t}(K', a) = \bigcup_{k \in K'} \hat{t}(k, a).$$

We can then define $\hat{t}: 2^K \times T^* \to 2^K$ by setting,

$$\hat{t}(K', ax) = \hat{t}(\hat{t}(K', a), x), \text{ for all } K' \subset K, a \in T, x \in T^*.$$

The set of strings accepted by the NFSA with ε-moves $M = (K, T, t, k_1, F)$, is then formally defined by

$$T(M) = \{x \in T^* \mid \hat{t}(\{k_1\}, x) \cap F \neq \varnothing\}.$$

If M is such an automaton then we can construct from M the NFSA $M' = (K, T, t', k_1, F')$ where $t'(k, a) = \hat{t}(k, a)$ and $F' = F$ if $R(k_1) \cap F = \varnothing$ and $F \cup \{k_1\}$ otherwise. M' has no ε-moves and it is not difficult to show that $T(M) = T(M')$. We thus have the result

Theorem 3.6

If L is accepted by a NFSA with ε-moves then L is a regular language.

The equivalent NFSA without ε-moves constructed from our example is given in Fig. 3.7.

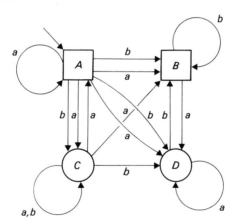

Figure 3.7

EXERCISES

1 Let L denote the set of strings in $\{0, 1\}^*$ such that every 0 has a 1 immediately to the right.
    (a) Construct a regular grammar generating L.
    (b) Construct a *deterministic* finite state automaton accepting L.
2 Let L be a regular set. Let $\mathrm{Pref}(L) = \{x \mid x$ is a prefix of a string in $L\}$. Show that $\mathrm{Pref}(L)$ is also regular. (Hint: use the fact that $L = T(M)$ for some DFSA, M.)
3 Write out the formal proofs for Theorem 3.1b.
4 Let $M = (\{k_1, k_2, k_3\}, \{a, b\}, t, k_1, \{k_3\})$ be a NFSA where $t(k_1, a) =$

$\{k_2, k_3\}$, $t(k_2, a) = \{k_1, k_2\}$, $t(k_3, a) = \{k_1, k_3\}$, $t(k_1, b) = \{k_1\}$, $t(k_2, b) = \varnothing$, $t(k_3, b) = \{k_1, k_2\}$. Find a deterministic automaton that accepts $T(M)$.

5   Construct a DFSA equivalent to the NFSA of Fig. 3.6.

6   A *homomorphism* $\theta: T_1^* \to T_2^*$ is a total function such that $\theta(\varepsilon) = \varepsilon$ and $\theta(xy) = \theta(x)\theta(y)$ for any $x, y \in T_1^*$.

   If $T_1 = \{a, b\}$, $T_2 = \{b, c\}$ and $\theta(a) = bc$, $\theta(b) = bb$, determine $\theta(ab)$ and $\theta(ba)$. Show that if L is a regular language and θ is an arbitrary homomorphism then $\theta(L)$ is a regular language.

7   Write out the formal proof of Theorem 3.6.

8   Use Theorem 3.6 to produce an alternative proof of Theorem 3.1a.

9   Describe a finite state automaton which will accept any word in the English alphabet beginning with '*un*' and ending with '*d*'. Use this FSA to write a PASCAL program which scans English text and counts the number of such words.

10   If every production in a grammar $G = (N, T, P, S)$ is either of the form $A \to Ba$ or of the form $A \to a, A, B \in N, a \in T$, show that there is an NFSA which accepts $L(G)$. (Hint: the production $A \to Ba$ corresponds to an arc labelled a from a node labelled B to a node labelled A.)

11   If every production in a grammar $G = (N, T, P, S)$ is either of the form $A \to xB$ or of the form $A \to x$, $A, B \in N$, $x \in T^*$, the grammar is called *right-linear*. Similarly, if every production is of the form $A \to Bx$ or of the form $A \to x, A, B \in N, x \in T^*$, the grammar is called *left-linear*. Show that $L \in T^*$ is generated by a right-linear grammar iff L is regular iff L is generated by a left-linear grammar.

Chapter 4

Regular Languages II

A drawing should have no unnecessary lines and a machine no unnecessary parts.

WILLIAM STRUNK, JR.
The Elements of Style

REGULAR EXPRESSIONS

Regular expressions are particularly neat ways of representing regular languages. The rules defining *regular expressions over T* can be summarized as follows:

(i) 0 represents the empty set and 1 represents $\{\varepsilon\}$;

(ii) if $L = \{x_1, x_2, \ldots, x_n\}$ is a finite set of strings where $x_i \in T^*, i = 1, \ldots, n$, then L is represented by $(x_1 + x_2 + \cdots + x_n)$;

(iii) if r_1 is a regular expression representing a regular language L_1 and r_2 is a regular expression representing a regular language L_2, then

$$(r_1 + r_2) \quad \text{represents } L_1 \cup L_2,$$

$$(r_1 \cdot r_2) \quad \text{represents } L_1 L_2,$$

$$(r_1^k) \quad \text{represents } L_1^k \, (k \geq 0)$$

and

$$(r_1^*) \quad \text{represents } L_1^*;$$

(iv) only those expressions defined by (i), (ii) and (iii) are regular expressions.

Parentheses in regular expressions can be omitted according to the rule that the unary operators have the highest priority, then $\cdot$ and lastly $+$. As with normal algebra, $(r_1 r_2)$ is commonly written for $(r_1 \cdot r_2)$.

Since every finite set of strings is a regular language and since regular languages are closed under union, set concatenation and Kleene closure, it follows that every regular expression over T describes a regular language in T^*. For example,

$$(a + b)^* ba(ba)^* \text{ describes } \{a, b\}^* \{ba\} \{ba\}^* = \{a, b\}^* \{ba\}^+$$

and

$$(a + ba^*b)^* + b \text{ describes } (\{a\} \cup \{b\} \{a\}^* \{b\})^* \cup \{b\}.$$

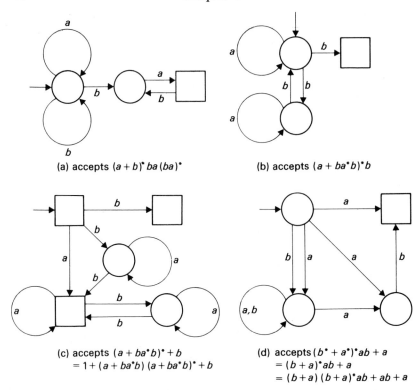

(a) accepts $(a + b)^* ba\,(ba)^*$

(b) accepts $(a + ba^*b)^*b$

(c) accepts $(a + ba^*b)^* + b$
$= 1 + (a + ba^*b)\,(a + ba^*b)^* + b$

(d) accepts $(b^* + a^*)^*ab + a$
$= (b + a)^*ab + a$
$= (b + a)\,(b + a)^*ab + ab + a$

Figure 4.1

It is usually fairly easy to construct a NFSA which accepts the language described by a given regular expression. However, it is also fairly easy to make a mistake! We illustrate some of the techniques you can use in Fig. 4.1a–4.1d. In these and other examples, we shall use R to denote the language represented by the regular expression, R.

   You will notice that in two of these examples, we have done a little manipulation to rewrite the regular expression in order to simplify the construction. In fact, without this rewriting it is very easy to get into difficulties. There is a whole algebra of regular expressions given by the set of identities $(a) - (p)$ and the two inference rules (q) and (r) of the following theorem. It has been shown that this set of identities together with these rules will enable you to prove the equivalence of any two regular expressions which describe the same regular set. The task of providing such a proof is not trivial, however, and we will be showing a better way of proving the equivalence of regular expressions later in this chapter.

Theorem 4.1

If Q, R, S are any regular expressions over T, then
(a) $Q + Q = Q, Q + 0 = Q,$
(b) $Q + R = R + Q,$
(c) $(Q + R) + S = Q + (R + S) = Q + R + S,$
(d) $(QR)S = Q(RS) = QRS,$
(e) $Q1 = 1Q = Q$ and $Q0 = 0Q = 0,$
(f) $(R + S)Q = RQ + SQ,$
(g) $Q(R + S) = QR + QS,$
(h) $Q^*Q^* = Q^*,$
(i) $(Q^*)^* = Q^*,$
(j) $QQ^* = Q^*Q,$
(k) $Q^* = 1 + Q + Q^2 + \cdots + Q^{k+1}Q^*,$ for any $k \geq 0,$
(l) $1^* = 1$ and $0^* = 1,$
(m) $(Q^* + R^*)^* = (Q^*R^*)^* = (Q + R)^*,$
(n) $(RQ)^*R = R(QR)^*,$
(o) $(Q^*R)^*Q^* = (Q + R)^*,$
(p) $(Q^*R)^* = (Q + R)^*R + 1$ and $(QR^*)^* = Q(Q + R)^* + 1,$
(q) $Q = R^*S$ implies $Q = RQ + S,$
(r) If $1 \notin R$ then $Q = RQ + S$ implies $Q = R^*S.$

Proof Most of these results are obvious once the reader associates $+$ with union and $\cdot$ with set concatenation. We will prove just the two inference rules by way of illustration.

(q) $Q = R^*S = (RR^* + 1)S$ [using (b) and (k)]

$\qquad\quad = RR^*S + S$ [using (e) and (f)]

$\qquad\quad = RQ + S.$

(r) $Q = RQ + S$ implies $Q = R(RQ + S) + S$

$\qquad\qquad\qquad\qquad\quad = R^2Q + RS + S$

$\qquad\qquad\qquad\qquad\quad = R^2(RQ + S) + RS + S$

$\qquad\qquad\qquad\qquad\quad = R^3Q + R^2S + RS + S$

$$\cdots$$

$\qquad\qquad\qquad\qquad\quad = R^{k+1}Q + (R^k + \cdots + R + 1)S$ for any $k \geq 0.$
Now, for any $x \in Q, |x| \leq k$ for some $k \geq 0.$ Since $1 \notin R.$ It follows that $x \notin R^{k+1}Q$ and hence $x \in (R^k + \cdots + R + 1)S,$ so $x \in R^*S.$ Thus $x \in Q$ implies $x \in R^*S.$ Conversely, if $x \in R^*S$ then $x \in (R^k + \cdots + R + 1)S$ for some $k \geq 0.$ Thus $x \in R^*S$ implies $x \in Q.$ Combining these arguments shows $Q = R^*S.$

We have observed that every regular expression describes a regular language. The converse of this result is also true and is given by the following theorem.

Theorem 4.2. Kleene's Theorem.

Every regular language in T^* can be described by a regular expression over T.

Proof Let L be a regular expression. Then $L = T(M)$ for some DFSA $M = (K, T, t, k_1, F)$. Assume $K = \{k_1, k_2, \ldots, k_n\}$. If $F = \{k_{\lambda 1}, k_{\lambda 2}, \ldots, k_{\lambda m}\}$ then $L = L_1 \cup L_2 \cup \ldots \cup L_m$ where L_i is the language accepted by $M_i = (K, T, t, k_1, \{k_\lambda\})$. Since we can represent the union operation using $+$ in regular expressions all we need to show is that each L_i can be represented by a regular expression. Thus, we need to show that the set of strings accepted by an arbitrary DFSA with one start state and one final state can be represented by a regular expression.

Consider $M = (K, T, t, k_1, F)$ where the labelling of the states is such that $K = \{k_1, k_2, \ldots, k_n\}$ and $F = \{k_n\}$. Denote by T_{ij}^l ($1 \le i, j \le n, 0 \le l \le n$) the language comprising all strings x such that both $t(k_i, x) = k_j$ and for all proper prefixes, y, of x, $t(k_i, y) \in \{k_m : m \le l\}$. (A proper prefix of $x \in T^*$ is any string $y \in T^+$ such that $x = yv$ for some $v \in T^+$. Thus y can be neither the empty string nor x itself.) We show by induction on l that T_{ij}^l can always be represented by a regular expression. Now, if $i \ne j$, T_{ij}^0 is 0 unless there are one or more arcs from node k_i to node k_j, in which case T_{ij}^0 is $a_1 + a_2 + \cdots + a_r$ where $a_1, a_2, \ldots, a_r$ are the labels on all such arcs. If $i = j$, T_{ii}^0 is 1 unless there are one or more arcs from node k_i to itself, in which case $T_{ii}^0 = 1 + a_1 + a_2 + \cdots + a_r$ where $a_1, a_2, \ldots, a_r$ are the labels on all such arcs. We have thus shown T_{ij}^l is a regular expression if $l = 0$. We can then show every T_{ij}^l is a regular expression using a simple induction argument based on the observation that $T_{ij}^l = T_{ij}^{l-1} + T_{il}^{l-1}(T_{ll}^{l-1})^* T_{lj}^{l-1}$, for all $1 \le l \le n$. Since $T(M) = T_{1n}^n$ the theorem is then proved.

If the observation used in this argument is not obvious to you, consider the labelled digraph representing M and any $x \in T_{ij}^l$. There is a path labelled x from the node labelled k_i to the node labelled k_j which goes via nodes labelled by elements of $\{k_1, k_2, \ldots, k_l\}$. The path must either not go via the node labelled k_l at all in which case $x \in T_{ij}^{l-1}$ or it does go via this node and say it then visits it $m \ge 1$ times. The path from the node labelled k_i to the node labelled k_j can be partitioned: (0) from node labelled k_i to node labelled k_l for the first visit, (1) from node labelled k_l and back to itself for a second visit, ... $(m - 1)$ from node labelled k_l and back to itself for the mth visit, (m) from node labelled k_l to the node labelled k_j. We can thus write $x = x_0 x_1 \ldots x_m$ where x_i is the label on the ith partition of the path. Now, $x_0 \in T_{il}^{l-1}, x_1, \ldots, x_{m-1} \in T_{ll}^{l-1}$ and $x_m \in T_{lj}^{l-1}$. Thus $x \in T_{il}^{l-1}(T_{ll}^{l-1})^* T_{lj}^{l-1}$. It is easy to see that any string in this set will be an element of T_{ij}^l so the equality follows.

MINIMIZATION

When we construct a DFSA which accepts some language L we would like to be able to have as few states as possible. Such a DFSA is called a *minimal*

DFSA and in this section we will show how to construct it and, moreover, prove that it is essentially unique.

You will recall from Chapter 1 that any equivalence relation on A divides A into a number of disjoint equivalence classes where we denote the equivalence class containing $a \in A$ by $\bar{a}$. The *index* of the equivalence relation is the number of these equivalence classes.

We will be focusing our attention on equivalence relations defined on T^*. Such an equivalence relation, R, is called *right invariant* if

$$xRy \text{ implies for all } z \in T^*, xzRyz.$$

Let L be some language in T^* and define the *relation associated with* L, R_L, by

$$xR_L y \text{ iff for all } z \in T^*, xz \in L \text{ exactly when } yz \in L.$$

R_L is an equivalence relation since it is reflexive, symmetric and transitive.

If $M = (K, T, t, k_1, F)$ is a DFSA then we can also define a *relation associated with* M, R_M. Two strings $x, y \in T^*$ are related by R_M iff they will both lead you from the start state of M to the same state, i.e.

$$xR_M y \text{ iff } t(k_1, x) = t(k_1, y).$$

Once more this is an equivalence relation and moreover it is right invariant. We will restrict our discussion for the moment to DFSAs with total transition functions. Then R_M will partition the whole of T^* into a number of disjoint equivalence classes. Each equivalence class comprises strings which get you from the start state to some particular state. Thus each equivalence class is very naturally associated with a state in K. Since there are only $\#(K)$ states there are only $\#(K)$ equivalence classes and hence R_M is of finite index.

Now, since R_M is right invariant, $xR_M y$ implies for all $z \in T^*, xzR_M yz$. Let L be the language accepted by M, i.e. $L = T(M)$. Then $xzR_M yz \Rightarrow t(k_1, xz) = t(k_1, yz) \Rightarrow t(k_1, xz) \in F$ iff $t(k_1, yz) \in F \Rightarrow xz \in L$ iff $yz \in L$. We have thus shown that $xR_M y$ implies $xR_L y$. Thus any equivalence class defined by R_M must lie wholly in an equivalence class defined by R_L. Since R_M partitions T^* into a finite number of equivalence classes, R_L must also be of finite index. Each equivalence class of R_L contains one or more equivalence classes of R_M so with each equivalence class of R_L we can associate a subset of the states of M. The subsets associated with distinct equivalence classes of R_L will be disjoint. If k, k' are two states in K associated with the same equivalence class of R_L then for all $z \in T^*, t(k, z) \in F$ iff $t(k', z) \in F$. In such a case we say that k and k' are *indistinguishable*.

Since the argument above is valid for any DFSA with a total function that accepts L it is apparent that any such DFSA must have $\geq n$ states where n is the index of R_L. Moreover, if $M = (K, T, t, k_1, F)$ and $M' =$

(K', T, t', k'_1, F') are two DFSAs each with n states accepting L then precisely one state of each machine can be associated with each equivalence class of R_L. This gives a natural bijection $\theta : K \to K'$ which can easily be shown to satisfy $\theta(k) = \theta(k') \Rightarrow \theta(t(k, a)) = \theta(t'(k', a)), \forall a \in T$. This bijection shows that, up to renaming of states, any DFSA with a total transition function that accepts L and has just n states is unique. We now need to show that there is at least one such automaton.

Say the equivalence classes defined by R_L are $\bar{x}_1, \bar{x}_2, \ldots, \bar{x}_n$. Then we can construct a DFSA, M_L, with input alphabet, T and with states $\{\bar{x}_1, \bar{x}_2, \ldots, \bar{x}_n\}$, start state $\bar{\varepsilon}$ and final states, F, where $\bar{x} \in F$ iff $x \in L$. The transition function is defined by setting $t(\bar{x}, a) = \bar{xa}$. Since R_L is right invariant, $x R_L y$ implies $xa R_L ya$ so this definition is consistent. Now, $x \in T(M)$ iff $t(\bar{\varepsilon}, \bar{x}) = \bar{x} \in F$ iff $x \in L$ so $T(M) = L$.

We have thus proved the following theorem.

Theorem 4.3. Myhill-Nerode Theorem

For any regular language L, there exists a DFSA with a total transition function which accepts L and has a number of states equal to the index of R_L, the relation associated with L.

Any state in the DFSA constructed by the Myhill-Nerode Theorem which does not lie on a path from the start state to a final state can be omitted together with all the arcs to or from that state. The DFSA remaining will be called the *minimal* DFSA *accepting L* and denoted by M_L.

Let $M = (K, T, t, k_1, F)$ be any DFSA accepting L which has a total transition function. We will describe an algorithm which computes M_L directly from L. Our task is to partition the states of M into disjoint subsets of indistinguishable states. We define relations $D_0, D_1, \ldots$ on K as follows. A state k is distinguishable from a state k' by a string of length 0, written $k D_0 k'$, iff either $k \in F$ and $k' \notin F$ or $k \notin F$ and $k' \in F$. Then, for $i > 0$, we define $k D_i k'$, k is distinguishable from k' by a string of length $\le i$ iff $k D_{i-1} k'$ or there exists $a \in T$ such that $t(k, a) D_{i-1} t(k', a)$. A state k is distinguishable from a state $k', k D k'$ iff there exists $i \ge 0$ such that $k D_i k'$. An easy induction argument shows that $k D_i k'$ iff there exists a string x of length $\le i$ such that either $t(k, x) \in F$ and $t(k', x) \notin F$ or $t(k, x) \notin F$ and $t(k', x) \in F$. Now, to compute D, we compute $D_0, D_1, D_2, \ldots$. When $D_r = D_{r+1}$ we know our computation can cease and $D_r = D$. If $m = \#(K)$ then there are only $m^2 - m$ pairs (k_i, k_j) where $i \ne j$. At worst, each D_{i+1} differs from D_i by just two of these pairs and since $D_0 \ne \emptyset$ we know $D = D_r$ for $r < (m^2 - m)/2$.

We will illustrate the technique using the DFSA given in Fig. 4.2. We represent each relation D_i by a 5×5 Boolean matrix whose j, k^{th} entry is T

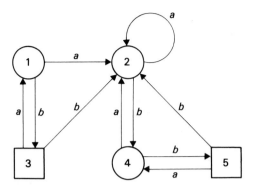

Figure 4.2

iff the state j is related to the state k by D_i. Since D_i is always symmetric and since $k D_i k$ for any k, we need only represent the part of the matrix above the diagonal. The sequence of matrices corresponding to $D_0, D_1 = D_2$ is given in Table 4.1; $1 D_1 2$ since $t(1,b) D_0 t(2,b)$ and $2 D_1 4$ since $t(2,b) D_0 t(4,b)$. This shows that states 1 and 4 are indistinguishable as are states 3 and 5.

Once all the indistinguishable states in a DFSA, M, are found, the construction of M_L follows easily. The states of M_L are sets of indistinguishable states. Say $K' \subset K$ is such a set, then we define the transition function of M_L, t_L, by $t_L(K', a) = K''$ where K'' is the set of indistinguishable states containing $t(k, a)$ for any $k \in K'$. The start state of M_L is the set of indistinguishable states containing the start state of M. The final states of M_L are those sets of states containing just final states of M. Applied to our example, this construction gives the minimal DFSA described in Fig. 4.3. In this case every node lies on a path from the start state to a final state so no nodes or arcs are removed.

In general, when describing a minimal DFSA, the nodes will not be labelled. We can then say the unlabelled DFSA is the unique minimal DFSA accepting L.

If the original DFSA has a partial transition function then we can add a new 'dummy' state, Δ, and construct an equivalent DFSA with a total function. If the above construction is then applied to this DFSA the set of

Table 4.1

$$
\begin{pmatrix}
\text{FTFT} \\
\text{.TFT} \\
\text{.TF} \\
\text{.T} \\
\\
D_0
\end{pmatrix}
\qquad
\begin{pmatrix}
\text{TTFT} \\
\text{.TTT} \\
\text{.TF} \\
\text{.T} \\
\\
D_1
\end{pmatrix}
$$

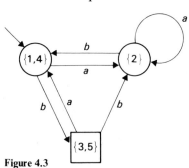

Figure 4.3

states indistinguishable from Δ cannot lie on a path from a start state to a final state and thus will not feature in the minimal DFSA.

ALGORITHMS FOR REGULAR GRAMMARS

Let M be an arbitrary regular language for which we have constructed a minimal DFSA, M_L, such that $T(M_L) = L$. Assume that M_L has the set of states, $K = \{k_1, \ldots, k_n\}$ where k_1 is the start state, and consider $z \in L$ of length $\geq n$. To be accepted by M_L, $t(k_1, z) \in F$. Since $|z| \geq n$, there must be some state $k \in K$ such that $z = wxy$ where $|x| \geq 1$ and $t(k_1, w) = k$, $t(k, x) = k$ and $t(k, y) \in F$. But then $t(k_1, wx^i y) \in F$ for $i \geq 0$ so $wx^i y \in L$ for $i \geq 0$. We have thus proved the following theorem.

Theorem 4.4

If L is a regular language and $z \in L$ is of length greater than or equal to the number of states in M_L, then $z = wxy$ where $|x| \geq 1$ and $wx^i y \in L$ for $i \geq 0$.

A corollary to this theorem is the fact that $L \neq \varnothing$ implies there exists $z \in L$ of length $< n$, the number of states in M_L. Thus a simple algorithm[1] to test if $L(G) = \varnothing$ or not is as follows: construct the minimal DFSA, M_L, for $L = L(G)$. If M_L has n states then $L = \varnothing$ iff M_L does not accept any string in T^* of length $< n$. Since there are only finitely many such strings, these can be tested in finite time. The above argument proves the following theories.

Theorem 4.5

The emptiness problem for regular grammars is solvable, i.e. given a regular grammar, G, there is an algorithm to determine whether or not $L(G) = \varnothing$.

　　　Similar results are as follows:

---

[1] An algorithm to solve a given problem, π, can be defined as a procedure which, given any instance of π as input, will always terminate outputting the desired solution.

Theorem 4.6

(a) The equivalence problem for regular grammars is solvable, i.e. given two regular grammars G_1, G_2, there is an algorithm to determine whether or not $L(G_1) = L(G_2)$.

(b) The finiteness problem for regular grammars is solvable, i.e. given a regular grammar, G, there is an algorithm to determine whether or not $L(G)$ is finite.

Proof (a) $L(G_1) = L(G_2)$ iff the minimal DFSAs constructed from G_1 and G_2 are identical up to renaming of states.

(b) Again the argument is based on the minimal DFSA, $M_L = (K, T, t, k_1, F)$, constructed to accept $L = L(G)$. If M_L has n states we know from Theorem 4.4 that L is infinite iff there exists $z \in L$ of length $\geq n$. Say there are such strings and let w be one of least length, i.e. $|w| \geq n$ and if $|z| \geq n$ then $|z| \geq |w|$. We will show $|w| < 2n$. Assume this is not the case; then we can write $w = w_1 w_2 w_3$ where $1 \leq |w_2| \leq n$ and where $t(k_1, w_1) = k$, $t(k, w_2) = k$, $t(k, w_3) \in F$ for some $k \in K$. Thus $t(k_1, w_1 w_3) \in F$ so $w_1 w_3 \in L$ but $|w_1 w_3| = |w| - |w_2| \geq 2n - n = n$ and $|w_1 w_3| < |w|$. This gives us our required contradiction. Thus our algorithm is simply to construct the minimal DFSA which accepts $L = L(G)$. If this DFSA has n states, we test to see if it accepts any string z such that $n \leq |z| < 2n$. There are finitely many such strings and L is infinite iff at least one such string is accepted.

The reader will note that the algorithms described in the proof of Theorem 4.5 and Theorem 4.6b do not really depend upon the accepting DFSA being minimal. The arguments can be applied to any DFSA setting n to be the number of states. The benefit of using the minimal DFSA comes from the fact that in such a case the value of n is as small as possible and hence the number of strings to be tested is as small as possible. These comments are summarized in our final theorem.

Theorem 4.7

The emptiness, equivalence and finiteness problems are solvable for deterministic (or nondeterministic) finite state automata.

EXERCISES

1 Describe deterministic finite state automata which accept
   (a) $a(ba + b)* + b$,
   (b) $(ab + b*)*ba + b$,
   (c) $((b*a)*ab*)*$.

2 Find a regular expression describing $T(M)$ where M is the nondeterministic finite state automaton described in Exercise 3.4.

3 Show that if $R_1, \ldots, R_n$ are regular expressions over T and $f(R_1, \ldots, R_n)$ is any function involving just the operators $+$, $\cdot$ and $*$ then
   (a) $f(R_1, \ldots, R_n) + (R_1 + \cdots + R_n)^* = (R_1 + \cdots + R_n)^*$;
   (b) $(f(R_1^*, \ldots, R_n^*))^* = (R_1 + \cdots + R_n)^*$.

4 Use Theorem 4.4 to show the following are not regular languages:
   (a) $\{a^n b^n \mid n \geq 0\}$,
   (b) $\{xx^r \mid x \in T^*\}$.

5 Find a deterministic finite state automaton which accepts the language L described by $(ab)^* + (a)(ba + a)^*$. Construct the minimal DFSA which accepts L. Use this DFSA to construct a DFSA which accepts $\bar{L} = \{a, b\}^* \backslash L$. Hence give a regular expression describing $\bar{L}$.

6 Let R_M be the relation associated with a DFSA $M = (K, T, t, k_1, F)$ such that $T(M) = L$. Let $\bar{x}, \bar{y}$ be two distinct equivalence classes of R_M. Show that if $t(k_1, x) = k$ and $t(k_1, y) = k'$ then $xR_L y$ iff k and k' are indistinguishable.

7 Examine your solutions to Exercise 4.1 and determine which (if any) of the DFSAs you have constructed are minimal.

Chapter 5

Context-free Languages

To show the form it seem'd to hide.

SIR WALTER SCOTT
The Lord of the Isles

We have seen in Chapter 2 that there are two equivalent definitions of context-free grammars. Firstly, we can define a context-free grammar (CFG) as a phrase structure grammar (N, T, P, S) where each production is of the form $A \to \alpha$, $A \in N$, $\alpha \in (N \cup T)^*$. This definition allows an arbitrary number of ε-productions to occur within the grammar. Alternatively, if $\varepsilon \notin L(G)$ we can restrict the productions in a CFG to be of the form $A \to \alpha$, $A \in N$, $\alpha \in (N \cup T)^+$ and thus have no ε-productions. Then, to allow for $\varepsilon \in L(G)$ we allow just one ε-production, $S \to \varepsilon$ and in that case insist that S does not appear as a substring of the right hand side of any production. We will generally opt for this second definition since it can make formal proofs a little easier.

If a language, L, is generated by a CFG then L is said to be a context-free language (CFL). Since any regular grammar is context-free, it follows that every regular language is a CFL. However, there are CFLs which are not regular. A simple example is the nonregular language $\{a^n b^n \mid n \geq 1\}$ which is generated by the CFG with productions

$$S \to aSb \mid ab$$

Let $G = (N, T, P, S)$ be any CFG and assume $L(G) \neq \varnothing$. For any $w \in T^+$ generated by G there is an associated derivation tree. We have defined the depth of a tree to be equal to the length of the longest path from the root node to a terminal node. Thus, if G_1 has productions

$$S \to AB$$
$$A \to aA \mid a$$
$$B \to bB \mid b$$

then the derivation tree for $a^3 b^2 \in L(G)$ given in Fig. 5.1 has depth four.

If the derivation tree for a CFG, $G = (N, T, P, S)$, has depth n then there must exist a path with nodes labelled $A_1, A_2, \ldots, A_n, a$ where $S = A_1, A_2, \ldots, A_n \in N$ and $a \in T$. If $n > \#(N)$, two or more of the nodes on this path must have the same label, say $A_i = A_j$ and $i < j$. We can construct a

Chapter 5

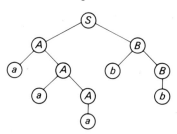

Figure 5.1

new derivation tree by replacing the tree rooted at A_i by the tree rooted at A_j. If we apply this argument repeatedly it follows that if there exists a derivation tree for $w \in L(G)$ with depth $> \#(N)$ then there exists a derivation tree for some $w' \in L(G)$ of depth $\leq \#(N)$. From this we conclude

Theorem 5.1

The emptiness problem for CFGs is solvable, i.e. for any CFG, $G = (N, T, P, S)$, there is an algorithm to determine whether or not $L(G) = \emptyset$. *Proof* The algorithm is simply to test if $S \to \varepsilon$ is a production in P. If so $L(G) \neq \emptyset$ since $\varepsilon \in L(G)$. Otherwise, we construct all the possible derivation trees *but only to a depth* $\#(N)$. These are finite in number and none of them corresponds to a derivation of a terminal string iff $L(G) = \emptyset$.

A production $A \to \alpha$ in a CFG $G = (N, T, P, S)$ is called *relevant* iff there exists a derivation of some $x \in L(G)$ which uses that production, i.e. iff $S \overset{*}{\Rightarrow} \alpha_1 A \alpha_2 \Rightarrow \alpha_1 \alpha \alpha_2 \overset{*}{\Rightarrow} x$ for some $x \in L(G)$. If a production in G is not relevant it is called *irrelevant* and we would like to be able to remove it. Now, for any $A \in N$, we can construct a new grammar $G_A = (N, T, P, A)$. If $L(G_A) = \emptyset$ then there is no possibility of generating a terminal string from A using productions in P. Thus from no sentential form of G containing A can we derive a terminal string. $L(G)$ will thus be unaffected if we remove from G all the productions with A on the left hand side or with A occurring on the right hand side. There may still be some irrelevant productions left in the grammar since there may be some $A \in N$ which can generate terminal strings but which can never appear in a sentential form. An argument similar to that used to prove Theorem 5.1 can be used to show that if A can occur in a sentential form then there is a sentential form containing A that can be derived by a partial derivation tree of depth $< \#(N)$. (The tree is a *partial* derivation tree because its leaves are not terminals.) By generating all such trees, we can check if any $A \in N$ cannot appear in a sentential form. If this is the case then any production involving A can be removed as irrelevant. From now on, we can thus assume that all productions in any CFG are relevant.

CHOMSKY NORMAL FORM

The format for productions in CFGs is really rather general and such generality makes formal proofs concerning CFGs overly difficult. Fortunately, we can constrain the productions quite significantly and yet maintain the power of the grammar.

Theorem 5.2. Chomsky Normal Form

Any ε-free CFL can be generated by a CFG in Chomsky Normal Form, i.e. one where all the productions are of the form

$$A \to BC, A, B, C \in N$$

or

$$A \to a, A \in N, a \in T$$

Proof If $L \subset T^*$ is an ε-free CFL then we can assume L is generated by a CFG $G = (N, T, P, S)$ which has no ε-productions. An equivalent CFG in Chomsky Normal Form (i.e. with all productions of the format specified in the theorem) can be constructed from G using the following algorithm.

Step 1: (Replace all productions of the form $A \to B$ where $A, B \in N$. We call productions of this form, *unit productions*). For any $A \in N$, let the set of unit productions with A on the left hand side be denoted by $U(A)$ and let the set of nonunit productions with A on the left hand side be denoted by $N(A)$. Then for each $A \in N$ such that $U(A) \neq \varnothing$, replace $U(A)$ by $\{A \to \alpha \mid A \overset{+}{\underset{G}{\Rightarrow}} B$ and $B \to \alpha$ is in $N(B)\}$.

Step 2: (Replace all productions whose right hand sides are strings of length > 1 and have terminals appearing as substrings. Such productions are called *secondary productions*). For each $a \in T$ appearing in the right hand side of a secondary production, introduce a new nonterminal A_a together with a new production $A_a \to a$. Any secondary production of the from $A \to X_1 X_2 \ldots . X_m$, $X_i \in N \cup T$ is then replaced by a production $A \to Y_1 Y_2 \ldots . Y_m$ where $Y_i = X_i$ if $X_i \in N$; otherwise $X_i = a$ for some $a \in T$ and $Y_i = X_a$. The augmented set of nonterminals is then denoted by N'.

Step 3: (Replace all productions whose right hand sides are strings of more than two nonterminals. Such productions are called *tertiary productions*). Any tertiary production of the form $A \to B_1 B_2 \ldots B_m$, $m > 2$, $B_1, B_2, \ldots, B_m \in N'$, is replaced by productions $A \to B_1 B_1', B_1' \to B_2 B_2', \ldots, B_{m-1}' \to B_{m-1} B_m$ where $B_1', \ldots, B_{m-1}'$ are new nonterminals which must not appear in any other production.

It should be clear that the grammar constructed from G using the above steps is equivalent to G and, moreover, is in Chomsky Normal Form. As an example of this construction, consider the CFG, G_2, with productions

$$S \rightarrow A \,|\, ABA$$
$$A \rightarrow aA \,|\, a \,|\, B$$
$$B \rightarrow bB \,|\, b$$

Step 1: $U(S)$ comprises $S \rightarrow A, U(A)$ comprises $A \rightarrow B$ while $U(B)$ is empty. Since $S \overset{+}{\Rightarrow} A$ and $S \overset{+}{\Rightarrow} B$ we replace $S \rightarrow A$ by $S \rightarrow aA \,|\, a \,|\, bB \,|\, b$ and since $A \overset{+}{\Rightarrow} B$ we replace $A \rightarrow B$ by $A \rightarrow bB \,|\, b$. The equivalent grammar then has productions

$$S \rightarrow aA \,|\, a \,|\, bB \,|\, b \,|\, ABA$$
$$A \rightarrow aA \,|\, a \,|\, bB \,|\, b$$
$$B \rightarrow bB \,|\, b$$

Step 2: Both a and b occur on the right-hand sides of secondary productions. We thus introduce new nonterminals A_a, A_b together with productions $A_a \rightarrow a$ and $A_b \rightarrow b$. The secondary productions are then rewritten resulting in the following set of equivalent productions.

$$S \rightarrow A_a A \,|\, a \,|\, A_b B \,|\, b \,|\, ABA$$
$$A \rightarrow A_a A \,|\, a \,|\, A_b B \,|\, b$$
$$B \rightarrow A_b B \,|\, b$$
$$A_a \rightarrow a$$
$$A_b \rightarrow b$$

Step 3: The only tertiary production is $S \rightarrow ABA$. This is replaced by productions

$$S \rightarrow AB'$$
$$B' \rightarrow BA$$

to obtain the final CFG which is in Chomsky Normal Form.

Let $L \subset T^*$ be an arbitrary CFL and let $L \backslash \{\varepsilon\}$ be generated by a Chomsky Normal Form CFG, G. If $x \in L(G)$ has a corresponding derivation tree of depth m then it can easily be proved that $|x| \leq 2^{m-1}$. The argument follows from the observation that any parent can have at most two children and parents of terminal nodes can only have one. As an illustration, an

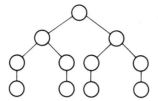

Figure 5.2

optimally large derivation tree of depth three has the structure described in Fig. 5.2.

We can now prove the following theorem.

Theorem 5.3

If L is a CFL then there exists integers l_1, l_2 such that for any $z \in L$ where $|z| > l_1, z$ may be written as $z = uvwxy$ where

(i) $|vwx| \le l_2$,

(ii) $vx \ne \varepsilon$, and

(iii) for each integer $i > 0$, $uv^iwx^iy \in L$.

Proof Let $L \backslash \{\varepsilon\}$ be generated by a Chomsky Normal Form grammar $G = (N, T, P, S)$. Let $n = \#(N)$ and put $l_1 = 2^{n-1}$ and $l_2 = 2^n$. Let $z \in L$ and $|z| > 2^{n-1}$. It follows that any derivation tree for z must contain a longest path, P, of length $> n$. There are more than $n + 1$ nodes in P of which only one is terminal. Thus there must be two nodes, N_1, N_2 in P both labelled with the same nonterminal where N_1 is the node nearer the root. There may be several such pairs of nodes in P but we will choose the pair with N_1 at the greatest depth. The only pair of nodes which are identically labelled and which lie on the path from N_1 to the terminal node of P will then be N_1 and N_2. Thus the length of this path is at most $n + 1$. Say N_1 and N_2 are both labelled A. Since P was a longest path in the derivation tree, the path from N_1 to the terminal node of P will be the longest path in the subtree rooted at N_1. Hence the depth of this subtree is at most $n + 1$ so it must represent the derivation of a terminal string from A of length at most 2^n. Call this string z_1. We have shown that $|z_1| \le 2^n$ and $A \overset{*}{\Rightarrow} z_1$. If T_2 is the subtree rooted at N_2 and w is the terminal string derived from it then we can write $z_1 = vwx$ where v, x cannot both be ε. This is because the first production used in the derivation of z_1 must be of the form $A \to BC$ for some $B, C \in N$ and no ε-productions are allowed. Now, z_1 is a substring of z and so we can write $z = uz_1y = uvwxy$. We have shown that there is a derivation $S \overset{*}{\Rightarrow} uAy \overset{*}{\Rightarrow} uvAxy \overset{*}{\Rightarrow} uvwxy$ where $|vwx| \le l_2$. Since $A \overset{*}{\Rightarrow} vAx \overset{*}{\Rightarrow} vwx$ it follows that $A \overset{*}{\Rightarrow} v^iwx^i$ for any $i > 0$. Hence $S \overset{*}{\Rightarrow} uAy \overset{*}{\Rightarrow} uv^iwx^iy$ is a valid derivation in G for any $i \ge 0$. Figure 5.3 provides a pictorial representation of the situation.

Chapter 5

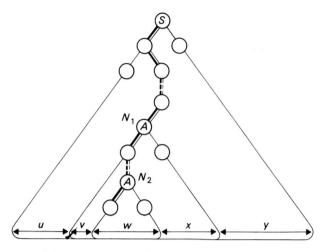

Figure 5.3

To demonstrate the argument of this theorem, consider the grammar, G_3, with productions

$$S \rightarrow AS \mid AB$$
$$A \rightarrow BS \mid a$$
$$B \rightarrow AA \mid b$$

Now, $l_1 = 4$ so consider the derivation tree for $a^3 b^2$ given in Fig. 5.4a. A path P of greatest length is indicated in this figure. There are four nonterminal nodes on this path and thus two of them must have the same label. In this example, there are two nodes labelled A. Let N_1 be the one nearer the root and N_2 be the other. T_1, the subtree rooted at N_1 gives a derivation $A \overset{*}{\Rightarrow} a^3 b$ and this is the z_1 of the theorem. T_2 is the subtree rooted at N_2 and this corresponds to a derivation $A \Rightarrow a$. Thus $z_1 = vwx$ where $v = a$, $w = a$, $x = ab$ and $z = uvwxy$ where $u = \varepsilon$ and $y = b$. The theorem states that for each integer $i \geq 0$, $uv^i wx^i y \in L$. Figures 5.4b and 5.4c give the derivation trees for the case $i = 0$ and $i = 2$ respectively. Figure 5.4b is constructed from 5.4a by replacing T_1 by T_2 and 5.4c is constructed from 5.4a by replacing T_2 by T_1.

Theorem 5.3 is particularly useful when you want to prove a language is *not* a CFL. For example consider the language $\{a^p \mid p$ is a prime number$\}$. If L were a CFL then a corollary of Theorem 5.3 would be the result that p is prime $\Rightarrow p + 2ki$ is prime for some k such that $0 < k \leq p$ and for all $i \geq 0$. This is clearly false so L cannot possibly be a CFL.

Let G be an arbitrary CFG written in Chomsky Normal Form. Assuming G has n nonterminals and setting $l_1 = 2^{n-1}$ and $l_2 = 2^n$, Theorem

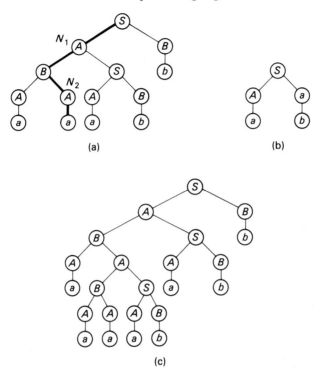

(a) (b)

(c)

Figure 5.4

5.3 tells us that $L(G)$ is infinite iff it contains a string of length $> l_1$. Assuming $L(G)$ is infinite, let z be the shortest string in $L(G)$ of length $> l_1$. We can show by contradiction that $l_1 < |z| \le l_1 + l_2$. Assume $|z| > l_1 + l_2$ but there is no shorter string contained in L with length $> l_1$. But, by Theorem 5.3, $z = uvwxy$ and $uwy \in L$ is a string of length $|z| - l_2 > l_1$. But $|uwy| < |z|$ which contradicts our assumption.

We have thus proved that $L(G)$ is infinite iff there exists $z \in L(G)$ such that $l_1 < |z| \le l_1 + l_2$. There are only finitely many strings $\in T^*$ which satisfy this length constraint. By generating all the sentential forms of G of length k, $l_1 < k \le l_1 + l_2$, we can see if any of them are terminal strings in $L(G)$. We thus have an algorithm to test whether $L(G)$ is infinite or not, i.e., we have proved the following.

Theorem 5.4

The finiteness problem is solvable for CFGs, i.e. there is an algorithm to determine whether an arbitrary CFG generates a finite or infinite language.

GREIBACH NORMAL FORM

When we discussed regular grammars in Chapter 3 we were fortunate in being able to find a particularly efficient way of answering the question 'is $x \in T^*$ an element of $L(G)$?' This is known as the *membership problem*. It is clearly also solvable for CFGs since we just need to generate all the sentential forms of G of length $|x|$. If none of these correspond to a derivation of x then $x \notin L(G)$ and otherwise $x \in L(G)$. Finding all these sentential forms is however not a very efficient way of answering the question and we will be spending a considerable amount of time finding better techniques. Since the actual construction of a derivation tree is so important in compiling we will also be interested in the associated question 'is $x \in T^*$ an element of $L(G)$ and if so, what is its derivation tree?' We will call this problem the *derivation problem*. Clearly if we can find an efficient algorithm to solve the derivation problem then we also have an efficient algorithm for the membership problem. So far, all we have established is that the problem is solvable.

In practice, the derivation problem can only be efficiently solved if certain restrictions are placed on the CFG. Depending upon the type of restriction certain algorithms have been designed to solve the derivation problem. Unfortunately these restrictions are such that not all CFLs can be so expressed. We will be discussing this further in Chapters 6, 7 and 8. Meanwhile, it is important that the reader learns to manipulate the productions of a grammar to change the format of the productions without changing the language generated. We have done a certain amount of this already in the previous section on Chomsky Normal Form.

The first technique to be discussed is very straightforward and is summarized in the theorem below. The proof is left to the reader.

Theorem 5.5

If $A \rightarrow \alpha_1 B\alpha_2$ is a production in a CFG, G and $B \rightarrow \beta_1|\beta_2|\ldots|\beta_k$ are all the productions with B on the left hand side then $A \rightarrow \alpha_1 B\alpha_2$ can be replaced by $A \rightarrow \alpha_1 \beta_1 \alpha_2 | \alpha_1 \beta_2 \alpha_2 | \ldots | \alpha_1 \beta_k \alpha_2$ without affecting $L(G)$.

The second result may not be so obvious so we will outline a proof. The theorem concerns the removal from a CFG of *left-recursive* productions, i.e. productions of the form $A \rightarrow A\alpha$, $A \in N$, $\alpha \in (N \cup T)^*$.

Theorem 5.6

If in a CFG, $A \rightarrow A\alpha_1|A\alpha_2|\ldots|A\alpha_m$ are all the left-recursive productions with A on the left-hand side and $A \rightarrow \beta_1|\beta_2|\ldots|\beta_n$ are the remaining productions with A on the left-hand side, then an equivalent grammar can be constructed by introducing a new nonterminal, A', and replacing all these productions by

$$A \rightarrow \beta_1 | \beta_2 | \ldots | \beta_n | \beta_1 A' | \beta_2 A' | \ldots | \beta_n A'$$
$$A' \rightarrow \alpha_1 | \alpha_2 | \ldots | \alpha_m | \alpha_1 A' | \alpha_2 A' | \ldots | \alpha_m A'$$

Proof In both cases the set of strings derivable from A using one or more of the productions is $\{\beta_1, \beta_2, \ldots, \beta_n\} \{\alpha_1, \alpha_2, \ldots, \alpha_m\}^*$.

As an example of the use of these two theorems, we will convert the productions of the grammar G_3 into productions of the form $A \rightarrow a\alpha$, $A \in N$, $a \in T$, $\alpha \in (N \cup T)^*$. When all the productions of a CFG are in this form, the CFG is said to be in *Greibach Normal Form*. For any ε-free CFL, L, it is always possible to construct a CFG in Greibach Normal Form to generate L. The general construction proceeds in the same way as this example.

Firstly, we rename the nonterminals of G_3 using A_1 for S, A_2 for A, A_3 for B. Our grammar thus has productions

$$A_1 \rightarrow A_2 A_1 | A_2 A_3$$
$$A_2 \rightarrow A_3 A_1 | a$$
$$A_3 \rightarrow A_2 A_2 | b$$

Our first step is to get every production of the form $A_i \rightarrow A_j\alpha$ to satisfy $j > i$. We have one production which does not satisfy this, viz. $A_3 \rightarrow A_2 A_2$. Applying Theorem 5.5 we replace this by

$$A_3 \rightarrow A_3 A_1 A_2 | a A_2$$

Now, we have introduced a left-recursive production and we use Theorem 5.6 to remove it. Our new set of productions is thus

$$A_1 \rightarrow A_2 A_1 | A_2 A_3$$
$$A_2 \rightarrow A_3 A_1 | a$$
$$A_3 \rightarrow a A_2 | b | a A_2 A_3' | b A_3'$$
$$A_3' \rightarrow A_1 A_2 | A_1 A_2 A_2'.$$

Every production with A_3 on the left-hand side is of the required form. $A_2 \rightarrow A_3 A_1$ can be rewritten using Theorem 5.5 and then so can $A_1 \rightarrow A_2 A_1 | A_2 A_3$. Then all productions with A_1, A_2 or A_3 on their left-hand sides will have the required format. The productions are

$$A_1 \rightarrow aA_2A_1A_1 | bA_1A_1 | aA_2A_3'A_1A_1 | bA_3'A_1A_1 | aA_1$$
$$| aA_2A_1A_3 | bA_1A_3 | aA_2A_3'A_1A_3 | bA_3'A_1A_3 | aA_3$$
$$A_2 \rightarrow aA_2A_1 | bA_1 | aA_2A_3'A_1 | bA_3'A_1 | a$$
$$A_3 \rightarrow aA_2 | b | aA_2A_3' | bA_3'$$
$$A_3' \rightarrow A_1A_2 | A_1A_2A_3'$$

Finally, the productions with A_3' on the left-hand side can also be rewritten using Theorem 5.5 to get

$$A_3' \rightarrow aA_2A_1A_1A_2 | bA_1A_1A_2 | aA_2A_3'A_1A_1A_2 | bA_3'A_1A_1A_2 | aA_1A_2$$
$$| aA_2A_1A_3A_2 | bA_1A_3A_2 | aA_2A_3'A_1A_3A_2 | bA_3'A_1A_3A_2 | aA_3A_2$$
$$| aA_2A_1A_1A_2A_3' | bA_1A_1A_2A_3' | aA_2A_3'A_1A_1A_2A_3'$$
$$| bA_3'A_1A_1A_2A_3' | aA_1A_2A_3' | aA_2A_1A_3A_2A_3' | bA_1A_3A_2A_3'$$
$$| aA_2A_3'A_1A_3A_2A_3' | bA_3'A_1A_3A_2A_3' | aA_3A_2A_3'$$

Thus this Greibach Normal Form grammar has thirty-nine productions! We now want to make sure that the construction we have used for this example will work in general. Firstly, we describe the steps we have used and then we will prove that they will always construct an equivalent Greibach Normal Form grammar.

Step 1: Let G be an arbitrary ε-free grammar. Convert G to an equivalent grammar, G', in Chomsky Normal Form.

Step 2: Rename the nonterminals in G' as $A_1, A_2, \ldots, A_m$ $(m \geq 1)$ where A_1 is the start symbol. Let $N = \{A_1, A_2, \ldots, A_m\}$.

Step 3: Apply the following algorithm to convert every production of G' with an A_i on the left-hand side to be either of the form $A_i \rightarrow a\alpha$, $a \in T$ or of the form $A_i \rightarrow A_j\alpha$ where $j > i$.

> *begin*
> *var i*: integer;
> $i := 0$;
> *while* $i \langle \rangle m$ *do*
>> *begin* $i := i + 1$;
>> *while* there exists a production of form $A_i \rightarrow A_j\alpha$, $j < i$ *do* substitute for A_j according to Theorem 5.5;
>> *if* there exist left-recursive productions with A_i on the left-hand side
>> *then* introduce a new nonterminal A_i' and use Theorem 5.6 to replace these left-recursive productions by an equivalent set of productions
>> *end*
> *end*

Step 4: Say N' denotes the new nonterminals introduced in Step 3.

Then, after Step 3 all productions of the grammar are of the form $A_i \rightarrow A_j \alpha$, $j > i$ and $\alpha \in (N \cup N' \cup T)^*$, $A_i \rightarrow a\alpha$, $a \in T, \alpha \in (N \cup N' \cup T)^*$ or $A_i' \rightarrow X\alpha$, $X \in (N \cup T)$, $\alpha \in (N \cup N' \cup T)^*$. Use the following algorithm to replace all productions which are of the first of these forms.

```
begin
var i: integer;
i: = m;
while i<>1 do
    begin i: = i − 1;
    while there exists a production of the form A_i → A_jα, j > i do sub-
        stitute for A_j according to Theorem 5.5
    end
end
```

Step 5: Remove productions of the form $A_i' \rightarrow A_j \alpha$ by simply substituting for A_j according to Theorem 5.5 The grammar will then be of the required format.

Clearly, after Step 2 the grammar will generate $L(G)$ if A_1 is taken as the start symbol. To prove Step 3 achieves its stated objective, we will show by induction that after i iterations of the main loop, the algorithm will have modified all the productions with A_k, $k \leq i$, on the left hand side. Certainly after no iterations the algorithm has modified no productions so the statement is correct for $i = 0$. Assume the statement is correct for $i < n$ and consider the nth iteration. If there are productions $A_n \rightarrow A_j \alpha$ where $j < n$ then Theorem 5.5 is used to replace A_j by the right hand sides of productions which have A_j on the left-hand side. Since $j < n$, the induction hypothesis states that these right-hand sides must start either with a terminal or with A_k where $k > j$. Any production of the first type is acceptable and only if there are productions of the second type where $k < n$ will the inner loop be re-entered. It is clear, however, that there can be at most $n - 1$ iterations of this inner loop and after this all productions with A_n on the left hand side will have right-hand sides starting with a terminal or a nonterminal, A_k, where $k \geq n$. Any left-recursive productions with A_n on the left hand side are then replaced so the hypothesis holds for $i = n$. Hence, by induction, the algorithm described in Step 3 achieves its objective since it exits when $i = m$ and then all productions are of the desired format. By considering the way Theorem 5.5 is applied in Step 3 it can be seen that the right-hand side of any production with an introduced nonterminal on the left-hand side must start with an element of $N \cup T$. The statement at the beginning of Step 4 can thus be confirmed. In particular, it follows that the right-hand side of a production with A_m on the left hand side must start with a terminal. Any production with A_{m-1} on the left-hand side starts either with a terminal or with A_m. Any occurrences of the type of production $A_{m-1} \rightarrow A_m \alpha$ can then be removed using Theorem 5.5. Then all productions with A_m or A_{m-1} on the left-hand side have right-hand side starting with a terminal. This process is repeated to get all productions with left-hand sides A_m, $A_{m-1}, \ldots, A_2, A_1$ to have right-hand sides starting with a terminal. A formal inductive argument can be used to show that after n iterations of the loop in Step 4, all productions with $A_m, A_{m-1}, \ldots, A_{m-n}$ on the left-hand sides must have right-hand sides starting with a terminal. Step 4 thus achieves its objective since the algorithm given terminates after $m-1$ iterations. Step 5 is trivially correct and thus the whole construction is valid. We have proved the following theorem.

Theorem 5.7. Greibach Normal Form

For every ε-free CFL, L, there exists a CFG, G, in Greibach Normal Form such that $L = L(G)$.

CFLs AS SOLUTIONS OF EQUATIONS

Consider again the CFG with productions

$$S \rightarrow AB$$
$$A \rightarrow aA \mid a$$
$$B \rightarrow bB \mid b.$$

With each nonterminal of the grammar we can associate the set of terminal strings which can be derived from it. Thus, we associate with A the set $\{a^n \mid n \geq 1\}$, with B the set $\{b^n \mid n \geq 1\}$ and with S the set $\{a^m b^n \mid m, n \geq 1\}$. In this section we will use the nonterminal symbol itself to denote the associated set and thus write $A = \{a^n \mid n \geq 1\}$, $B = \{b^n \mid n \geq 1\}$ and $S = \{a^m b^n \mid m, n \geq 1\}$. From the productions of the grammar we know that the sets S, A, B must satisfy the system of equations

$$S = AB$$
$$A = \{a\} A \cup \{a\}$$
$$B = \{b\} B \cup \{b\}$$

Such equations can have an infinite number of possible solutions. For example, although one solution of

$$A = A \cup \{a\}$$

is $\{a\}$, any set containing a will also be a solution. These other solutions are not the ones you would naturally associate with the equation. The theory we will introduce will associate a unique 'least' solution with any system of equations.

Consider the following system of equations.

$$X_1 = f_1(X_1, X_2, \ldots, X_n)$$
$$X_2 = f_2(X_1, X_2, \ldots, X_n)$$
$$\ldots$$
$$\ldots$$
$$\ldots$$
$$X_n = f_n(X_1, X_2, \ldots, X_n)$$

where each $f_i(X_1, X_2, \ldots, X_n)$ is constructed from finite sets of strings in T^* and the variables $X_1, X_2, \ldots, X_n$ using the operations of union and set concatenation only. Such a system of equations will be called a *system of set equations over* T^*. We will write X for the n-tuple $(X_1, X_2, \ldots, X_n)$ and the system of set equations as

$$X = f(X).$$

A solution to $X = f(X)$ is any n-tuple of sets in T^*, $S = (S_1, S_2, \ldots, S_n)$, which satisfies $S = f(S)$. If $T = (T_1, T_2, \ldots, T_n)$ we will write $S \subset T$ iff $S_1 \subset T_1$, $S_2 \subset T_2, \ldots, S_n \subset T_n$. The following theorem shows that any system of set equations over T^* has a unique 'least' solution.

Theorem 5.8

The system of equations $X = f(X)$ has a solution

$$S = \bigcup_{i=1}^{\infty} f^i(\emptyset)$$

and moreover if T is any other solution $S \subset T$.

Proof (Outline) $\emptyset$ denotes the n-tuple $(\emptyset, \emptyset, \ldots, \emptyset)$ and so by definition, $\emptyset \subset f(\emptyset)$. Using the result of Exercise 1.11, it can be easily shown for the functions under consideration that if $A \subset B$ then $f(A) \subset (B)$. Thus, $f(\emptyset) \subset f(f(\emptyset)) = f^2(\emptyset)$. Continuing with this argument we see that $\emptyset \subset f(\emptyset) \subset f^2(\emptyset) \subset \ldots$ forms a nondecreasing sequence. Let

$$S = \bigcup_{i=1}^{\infty} f^i(\emptyset)$$

be the limit of this sequence then it can be shown that $f(S) = S$ so S is a solution to the system of equations.

If T is some other solution then $T = f(T)$. Now, by definition $\emptyset \subset T$ so $f(\emptyset) \subset f(T) = T$. Continuing this argument we can show that $f^i(\emptyset) \subset T$ for all $i \geq 0$. Thus

$$\bigcup_{i=1}^{\infty} f^i(\emptyset) \subset T, \quad \text{i.e.} \quad S \subset T.$$

Given any context-free grammar $G = (N, T, P, S)$ there is an associated system of set equations over $T*$ and vice versa. Moreover if $S = (S_1, S_2, \ldots, S_n)$ is the unique least solution of this system of equations and if the first equation in the system corresponds to the productions in P with S on the left-hand side, then $L(G) = S_1$. Let us apply this argument to the system of equations

$$S = AB = f_1(S, A, B)$$
$$A = \{a\}\, A \cup \{a\} = f_2(S, A, B)$$
$$B = \{b\}\, B \cup \{b\} = f_3(S, A, B).$$
$$f(\varnothing) = (f_1(\varnothing), f_2(\varnothing), f_3(\varnothing)) = (\varnothing, \{a\}, \{b\}),$$
$$f^2(\varnothing) = (f_1(\varnothing, \{a\}, \{b\}), f_2(\varnothing, \{a\}, \{b\}), f_3(\varnothing, \{a\}, \{b\}))$$
$$= (\{ab\}, \{a, aa\}, \{b, bb\}),$$

and

$$f^3(\varnothing) = f(\{ab\}, \{a, aa\}, \{b, bb\})$$
$$= (\{ab, aab, abb, aabb\}, \{a, aa, aaa\}, \{b, bb, bbb\}).$$

An inductive argument can be used to show that

$$f^i(\varnothing) = (\{a^m b^n | i > m, n \geq 1\}, \{a^m | i \geq m \geq 1\}, \{b^n | i \geq n \geq 1\})$$

and hence the limit

$$\bigcup_{i=1}^{\infty} f^i(\varnothing) = (\{a^m n^n | m, n \geq 1\}, \{a^m | m \geq 1\}, \{b^n | n \geq 1\}).$$

Hence $L(G) = \{a^m b^n | m, n \geq 1\}$.

Expressing CFLs as solutions of systems of set equations can often lead to a better understanding of the nature of the language. Also after only a finite number of steps in the chain $\varnothing \subset f(\varnothing) \subset \ldots$ all the strings on $L(G)$ of a given length will be found. Thus this approach can be used to solve the membership problem.

EXERCISES

1 Describe an algorithm which given an arbitrary CFG, G, and an integer $k \geq 0$ will generate all the derivation trees for G of depth k.

2 If L is a CFL, show that the Kleene closure of L, L^*, and the reversal of L, $L' = \{x^r | x \in L\}$, are also CFLs.

3 If L_1, L_2 are CFLs show that $L_1 \cup L_2$ and $L_1 L_2$ are also CFLs.

4 Construct a CFG in Chomsky Normal Form which generates arithmetic expressions over $\{a, b, c\}$.

5 Which of the following are CFLs and which are not?
   (a) $\{a^i b^j c^k | 0 \leq i < j < k\}$,

(b) $\{a^i b^j c^k | 0 \le i = j = k\}$,

(c) $\{a^i b^j c^k | 0 \le i = j, 0 \le k \text{ and } i \ne k\}$,

(d) $\{a^i b^j c^k | 0 \le i = j, 0 \le k\}$.

6 Show that if $L \subset T_1^*$ is a CFL and $\phi : T_1^* \to T_2^*$ is a homomorphism then $\phi(L)$ is a CFL.

7 Write out the formal proofs of Theorems 5.5 and 5.6.

8 State and prove a theorem analogous to Theorem 5.6 which can be used to remove from a CFG all right-recursive productions (i.e. ones of the form $A \to \alpha A$, $A \in N$, $\alpha \in (N \cup T)^*$).

9 Convert to Greibach Normal Form the grammar with productions

$$A_1 \to A_2 A_3$$
$$A_2 \to A_3 A_1 | b$$
$$A_3 \to A_1 A_2 | a$$

10 Consider the CFG, G, with productions

$$S \to AS | BS | a$$
$$A \to BB | a$$
$$B \to AA | b$$

Express $L(G)$ as a solution to a system of set equations and use this system to determine all $x \in L(G)$ of length less than five.

11 Use your solution to Exercise 5.5 to construct CFLs, L_1, L_2 such that $L_1 \cap L_2$ is *not* a CFL.

12 Use your solution to Exercise 5.11 to show that there is a CFL, $L \subset T^*$ such that its complement $\bar{L} = T^* \setminus L$ is *not* a CFL.

Chapter 6

Pushdown Automata

If anyone anything lacks
He'll find it all ready in stacks.

SIR WILLIAM SCHWENCK GILBERT
The Sorcerer

The finite state automata which we studied in Chapters 3 and 4 provided us with a particularly useful and simple way of handling regular languages. In this chapter, we will describe the corresponding automata for context-free languages. This is an important first step towards the design and implementation of practical, efficient parsers and hence very relevant to the potential compiler writer.

The automaton we require is equipped with a memory in the form of a stack. A *stack* is a last-in, first-out linear storage device familiar to all but the most novice of computer scientists. One end of the stack is called the *top* and the other end is called the *bottom*. There are two primitive operations that can be performed on a stack, PUSH and POP. PUSH takes an item and places it on the top of the stack. POP, on the other hand, removes an item from the top of the stack and delivers it as a result (see Fig. 6.1). For our purposes, the items on the stack will be symbols of a prescribed alphabet, V, and the stack will also have an unlimited storage capacity. This second condition ensures that it always be possible to perform a PUSH operation, i.e. that we can never get an *overflow* situation. However, for POP to deliver a result, it is, of course, necessary to have at least one symbol on the stack; if POP is applied to an *empty* stack, i.e. one with no symbols stored in it, the resulting failure situation is called an *underflow*.

If V denotes the set of symbols which can appear on the stack then the contents of the stack can be represented by a string in V^*, with the head of

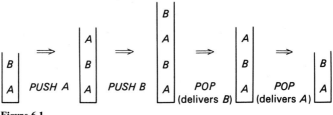

Figure 6.1

70

the string denoting the symbol at the top of the stack. To achieve this, the symbols in the stack from top to bottom are written as a string from left to right. Thus, the example in Fig. 6.1 can be written as $BA \Rightarrow ABA \Rightarrow BABA \Rightarrow ABA \Rightarrow BA$. The empty stack is represented by the empty string, ε. The primitive stack operations, PUSH and POP, can now be formally defined as functions on strings.

$$\text{PUSH}(A, X) = AX$$

defines the action of pushing $A \in V$ on a stack with contents $X \in V^*$.

$$\text{POP}_1(X) = \begin{cases} \text{undefined} & \text{if } X = \varepsilon \text{(underflow)}, \\ A & \text{if } X = AY, A \in V, Y \in V^*, \end{cases}$$

defines the symbol delivered by a POP operation applied to a stack with contents X.

$$\text{POP}_2(X) = \begin{cases} \text{undefined} & \text{if } X = \varepsilon \text{(underflow)} \\ Y & \text{if } X = AY, A \in V, Y \in V^*, \end{cases}$$

defines the condition of the stack initially with contents X after a *POP* operation has been performed upon it.

NONDETERMINISTIC PUSHDOWN AUTOMATA

A nondeterministic pushdown automaton (NPDA) can be loosely described as a nondeterministic finite state automaton equipped with a stack, the top element of which can influence the transition function. In a NFSA, the set of possible next states is determined from the current state and the input symbol. In a NPDA, the set of possible next states depends upon the current state, the input symbol and the symbol which is popped off the top of the stack. At the same time as changing to a new state, the NPDA may push any finite number of symbols onto the stack.

Formally, a *nondeterministic pushdown automaton* (NPDA) is a 7-tuple, $M = (K, T, V, p, k_1, A_1, F)$ where
(a) K is a finite set of *states*,
(b) T is a finite *input alphabet*,
(c) V is a finite alphabet of *stack symbols* (elements of which we will usually write as upper case letters toward the beginning of the alphabet and possibly subscripted),
(d) p is a total function $K \times V \times (T \cup \{\varepsilon\})$ to finite subsets of $K \times V^*$, called the *pushdown function*,
(e) $k_1 \in K$ is a designated *start state*,
(f) $A_1 \in V$ is a designated *start symbol* which is initially the only symbol on the stack,
(g) $F \subset K$ is a set of *final states*.

The *configuration* of an NPDA, $M = (K, T, V, p, k_1, A_1, F)$, at any time can be described by an ordered pair in $K \times V^*$. The first element in the ordered pair gives the current state of the automaton and the second element gives the current stack contents. If an NPDA, M, is in configuration c, we will define the *transition function* t_M such that $t_M(c, x)$ denotes the set of configurations in which M can be after an input of $x \in T^*$ has been processed. We first define $t_M : (K \times V^*) \times (T \cup \{\varepsilon\}) \to 2^{K \times V^*}$ to describe just one step of the automaton and then extend t_M to our desired objective.

If a single application of the pushdown function, p, can cause M to change from configuration $c = (k, AX), k \in K, A \in V, X \in V^*$ to configuration $c' = (k', YX), k' \in K, Y, X \in V^*$ given an input $a \in T \cup \{\varepsilon\}$, we want $t_M(c, a)$ to contain c'. We thus define t_M such that $t_M((k, AX), a)$ contains (k', YX) iff $p(k, A, a)$ contains (k', Y).

We should note here that $t_M(c, \varepsilon)$ always contains c by convention. It will only contain other configurations if M can move with no input from configuration c, i.e. if $c = (k, AX)$ is such that $p(k, A, \varepsilon) \neq \varnothing$. Such a move will be called an *ε-move*.

The first step in the definition of t_M is completed by observing that if the stack is empty then no move is possible. Thus

$$t_M((k, \varepsilon), a) = \varnothing \qquad \text{for all } k \in K, a \in T$$

and

$$t_M((k, \varepsilon), \varepsilon) = \{(k, \varepsilon)\} \qquad \text{for all } k \in K.$$

Now, we extend t_M to the required function $(K \times V^*) \times T^* \to 2^{K \times V^*}$ in the obvious way. If $k \in K$, $X \in V^*$, $a_1, a_2, \ldots, a_n \in T \cup \{\varepsilon\}$, then

$$t_M((k, X), a_1 a_2 \ldots a_n) \text{ contains } (k', X'), k' \in K, X' \in V^*$$
$$\text{iff } t_M((k, X), a_1) \text{ contains } (k_2, X_2),$$
$$t_M((k_2, X_2), a_2) \text{ contains } (k_3, X_3),$$

$$. \quad . \quad .$$
$$. \quad . \quad .$$
$$. \quad . \quad .$$

$$t_M((k_n, X_n), a_n) \text{ contains } (k', X')$$

for some $k_2, \ldots, k_n \in K, X_2, \ldots, X_n \in V^*$. Note that some of these a_i's may be ε if M can make ε-moves.

Now, $T(M)$, the *set of strings accepted by the NPDA, M*, can be defined.

$$T(M) = \{x \in T^* | t_M((k_1, A_1), x) \text{ contains some element of } F \times V^*\}$$

Thus $T(M)$ is the set of strings which when input can cause the initial configuration to change to a configuration with the automaton in a final state.

If it is clear from context to which NPDA we are referring, the subscript, M, can be dropped from the transition function, t_M.

As an example, we will construct an NPDA, M_1, such that $T(M_1) = \{xx^r | x \in \{a, b\}^*\}$. The technique used is to remember the first half of the string by storing it on the stack. When the second half of the string is processed we simply check that the incoming symbol matches the symbol popped off the top of the stack. Unfortunately, since we process the input one symbol at a time and we do not know the total length of the input until it has all been processed, we cannot tell when to stop pushing the incoming symbols onto the stack and start the matching process. For this reason, the automaton has to be nondeterministic. When pushing symbols, we remain in the start state, k_1. At any time, we can start the matching process by entering state k_2 but then no more pushing can take place. We set $M_1 = (\{k_1, k_2, k_3\}, \{a, b\}, \{a, b, \dashv\}, p, k_1, \dashv, \{k_3\})$ where $\dashv$ acts as a marker for the bottom of the stack. The pushdown function, p, is defined as below (with this and future examples, we adopt the convention that when describing the pushdown function associated with an NPDA, the rules for those arguments which yield the empty set will be omitted).

$$p(k_1, a, a) = \{(k_1, aa), (k_2, \varepsilon)\},$$
$$p(k_1, b, a) = \{(k_1, ab)\},$$
$$p(k_1, a, b) = \{(k_1, ba)\},$$
$$p(k_1, b, b) = \{(k_1, bb), (k_2, \varepsilon)\},$$
$$p(k_1, \dashv, a) = \{(k_1, a \dashv)\},$$
$$p(k_1, \dashv, b) = \{(k_1, b \dashv)\},$$
$$p(k_2, a, a) = \{(k_2, \varepsilon)\},$$
$$p(k_2, b, b) = \{(k_2, \varepsilon)\},$$
$$p(k_2, \dashv, \varepsilon) = \{(k_3, \varepsilon)\}.$$

The reader should satisfy himself that $T(M_1) = \{xx^r | x \in \{a, b\}^*\}$. As an illustration, consider $t((k_1, \dashv), abba)$. This can yield any configuration in $\{(k_1, abba \dashv), (k_2, \dashv), (k_3, \varepsilon)\}$ and hence $abba \in T(M_1)$.

By Theorem 3.3, every regular language $L \subset T^*$ can be accepted by some NFSA, $M = (K, T, t, k_1, F)$. From this NFSA we can construct a NPDA $M' = (K, T, \{\dashv\}, p, k_1, \dashv, F)$ such that $T(M') = L$. M' simulates the action of M by essentially ignoring the contents of its stack. To achieve this we simply define p by

$$p(k, \dashv, a) \text{ contains } (k', \dashv) \text{ iff } k' \in t(k, a).$$

Thus the stack contents remains at $\dashv$ throughout the moves made by M'. Clearly, $x \in T(M')$ iff $t_{M'}((k_1, \dashv), x) \cap (F \times \{\dashv\}) \neq \varnothing$ iff $t(k_1, x) \cap F \neq \varnothing$ iff $x \in T(M)$ iff $x \in L$.

The above argument proves that every regular language can be accepted by some NPDA. By our example, we also know that an NPDA can be constructed to accept a language that is not regular, viz $\{xx^r | x \in \{a, b\}^*\}$. Thus we know that NPDAs accept a strictly greater class of languages than FSAs. In fact, we will be showing that the languages they accept are precisely the context-free languages. The reader may be wondering whether the nondeterministic nature of these automata is absolutely essential. Unfortunately, it is—although deterministic and nondeterministic FSAs accept the same class of languages, this is not true of pushdown automata. Nondeterminism can be shown to be essential in the recognition of $\{xx^r | x \in \{a, b\}^*\}$. We will be returning to the topic of determinism later in this chapter.

NPDAs AS ACCEPTORS FOR CFL'S

The main result in this chapter is that NPDAs are the acceptors for CFLs. This means that for every CFL, L, there exists an NPDA which accepts that language and that, conversely, every language accepted by an NPDA is necessarily context-free. Before outlining the proof of these results we will consider an example to show how an NPDA can be constructed to accept simple arithmetic expressions.

Let $G = (N, T, P, E)$ be the CFG where $N = \{E, T, F\}$, $T = \{a, b, c, (,), +, -, \times, /\}$ and P consists of

$$E \to T | E + T | E - T$$
$$T \to F | T \times F | T/F$$
$$F \to a | b | c | (E)$$

From the discussion in Chapter 2, we know that every $x \in L(G)$ can be generated by a leftmost derivation. The NPDA which we construct to accept $L(G)$ will simulate such leftmost derivations on its stack. Initially, the stack contents is set to be $E \dashv$ where $\dashv$ is a special bottom-of-stack marker. Any of the productions $E \to T, E \to E + T, E \to E - T$ can then be applied to get a new stack contents of $T \dashv, E + T \dashv$ or $E - T \dashv$ respectively. At each move of the automaton the top stack symbol is popped. If it is a nonterminal symbol then it can be expanded using some production; the right-hand side of the production is then pushed back onto the stack. However, if it is a terminal symbol, for the process to continue, it must match the next input symbol.

Thus, we define $M = (K, T, V, p, k_1, \dashv, \{k_3\})$ where

$$K = \{k_1, k_2, k_3\},$$
$$V = N \cup T \cup \{\dashv\},$$

and p is defined by

$$p(k_1, \dashv, \varepsilon) = \{(k_2, E \dashv)\},$$

$$p(k_2, E, \varepsilon) = \{(k_2, T), (k_2, E + T), (k_2, E - T)\},$$
$$p(k_2, T, \varepsilon) = \{(k_2, F), (k_2, T \times F), (k_2, T/F)\},$$
$$p(k_2, F, \varepsilon) = \{(k_2, a), (k_2, b), (k_2, c), (k_2, (E))\},$$
$$p(k_2, a, a) = \{(k_2, \varepsilon)\}, p(k_2, b, b) = \{(k_2, \varepsilon)\},$$
$$p(k_2, c, c) = \{(k_2, \varepsilon)\},$$
$$p(k_2, +, +) = \{(k_2, \varepsilon)\}, p(k_2, -, -) = \{(k_2, \varepsilon)\},$$
$$p(k_2, \times, \times) = \{(k_2, \varepsilon)\}, p(k_2, /, /) = \{(k_2, \varepsilon)\},$$
$$p(k_2, (, () = \{(k_2, \varepsilon)\}, p(k_2,),)) = \{(k_2, \varepsilon)\},$$
$$p(k_2, \dashv, \varepsilon) = \{(k_3, \varepsilon)\},$$

The state k_1 is used to initialize the stack to $E \dashv$ and the state k_3 can only be entered once the stack contains just $\dashv$. Thus, the simulation of the leftmost derivation is done whilst the automaton is in state k_2. In Table 6.1, a sequence of configurations of M is shown to illustrate the fact that $a \times (b + c)$ is accepted.

To design an efficient parser for arithmetic expressions based on this

Table 6.1

	Sequence of Configurations	
Remaining input	State	Stack contents
$a \times (b + c)$	k_1	$\dashv$
$a \times (b + c)$	k_2	$E \dashv$
$a \times (b + c)$	k_2	$T \dashv$
$a \times (b + c)$	k_2	$T \times F \dashv$
$a \times (b + c)$	k_2	$F \times F \dashv$
$a \times (b + c)$	k_2	$a \times F \dashv$
$\times (b + c)$	k_2	$\times F \dashv$
$(b + c)$	k_2	$F \dashv$
$(b + c)$	k_2	$(E) \dashv$
$b + c)$	k_2	$E) \dashv$
$b + c)$	k_2	$\neq + T) \dashv$
$b + c)$	k_2	$T + T) \dashv$
$b + c)$	k_2	$F + T) \dashv$
$b + c)$	k_2	$b + T) \dashv$
$+ c)$	k_2	$+ T) \dashv$
$c)$	k_2	$T) \dashv$
$c)$	k_2	$F) \dashv$
$c)$	k_2	$c) \dashv$
$)$	k_2	$) \dashv$
ε	k_2	$\dashv$
ε	k_3	ε

automaton is not an easy task, however. The problem is that three of the above rules for p give a choice for the next move. If $x \in T(M)$ then we know that there is *some* sequence of configurations that will guarantee that M accepts x but there are going to be many valid sequences of moves that will not lead to the acceptance of x. In Chapters 7 and 8, we will show that if a grammar generating a language has certain properties then the NPDA constructed from it will not put us in this predicament. In such cases efficient parsers can be constructed.

Theorem 6.1

If L is a CFL then there exists a NPDA, M, such that $L = T(M)$.
Proof (outline)   Let $L \subset T^*$ be generated by the CFG $G = (N, T, P, S)$. We define

$$M = (K, T, V, p, k_1, \dashv, \{k_3\}) \text{ such that}$$
$$K = \{k_1, k_2, k_3\},$$
$$V = N \cup T \cup \{\dashv\}, \dashv \notin N \cup T,$$

and where p is defined by

$$p(k_1, \dashv, \varepsilon) = \{(k_2, S \dashv)\},$$
$$p(k_2, A, \varepsilon) = \{(k_2, \alpha) | A \rightarrow \alpha \text{ is in } P\}, \text{ for all } A \in N,$$
$$p(k_2, a, a) = \{(k_2, \varepsilon)\}, \text{ for all } a \in T,$$

and

$$p(k_2, \dashv, \varepsilon) = \{(k_3, \varepsilon)\}.$$

The construction ensures that for $x \in T^*$, $\alpha \in (N \cup T)^*$, $S \overset{*}{\Rightarrow} x\alpha$ is a leftmost derivation iff $t((k_1, \dashv), x)$ contains $(k_2, \alpha \dashv)$. Hence $x \in L(G)$ iff $S \overset{*}{\Rightarrow} x$ iff $t((k_1, \dashv), x)$ contains $(k_2, \dashv)$ iff $t((k_1, \dashv), x)$ contains $(k_3, \dashv)$ iff $x \in T(M)$.

The converse of Theorem 6.1 is also true, i.e. every language accepted by a NPDA is necessarily context-free. However, before we can prove this, we need a result concerning NPDAs. Let $M = (K, T, V, p, k_1, A_1, F)$ be an arbitrary NPDA. We construct from M a new NPDA, $M' = (K', T, V', p', k'_1, \dashv, F')$ such that

$$K' = K \cup \{k'_1, k'_2\} \quad \text{where } k'_1, k'_2 \notin K,$$
$$V' = V \cup \{\dashv\} \quad \text{where } \dashv \notin V,$$

p' is the same as p with the exception of the addition of the following rules concerning the new states k'_1, k'_2 and new stack symbol, $\dashv$,

$$p'(k'_1, \dashv, \varepsilon) = \{(k_1, A_1 \dashv)\},$$
$$p'(k, A, \varepsilon) = \{(k'_2, \varepsilon)\}, \text{ for all } A \in V', k \in F,$$

and

$$p'(k'_2, A, \varepsilon) = \{(k'_2, \varepsilon)\}, \text{ for all } A \in V',$$
$$F' = \{k'_2\}.$$

The first of the new rules is designed to place a bottom-of-stack marker, $\dashv$, on the stack before M' simulates the action of M. Then, if M' ever reaches a state in F there must be at least one symbol left on the stack. The second type of introduced rule can then be used by M' to enter k'_2 without necessitating any further input. Since $k'_2 \in F'$ it should be clear that $T(M) = T(M')$. M' has only the one final state and once M' enters this state the third type of rule can be used to clear the stack. We thus have

Theorem 6.2
If L is accepted by some NPDA, M, then L is accepted by a NPDA, M', which has only one final state and in which that automaton can clear the stack without further input. Moreover, this final state is the only state in which the stack can be cleared.

We can now prove our second major result.

Theorem 6.3
If $L = T(M)$ for some NPDA, M, then L is a CFL.
Proof (outline) We can assume that L is accepted by a NPDA with the properties described in Theorem 6.2. The states can be labelled $k_1, k_2, \ldots, k_n$ where k_1 is the start state and k_n is the only final state. Let $M = (\{k_1, k_2, \ldots, k_n\}, T, V, p, k_1, A_1, \{k_n\})$ be this NPDA accepting L. We need to construct from M a CFG, G, such that $T(M) = L(G)$.

For each $A \in V$, we use the nonterminal symbol A^{ij} in the constructed grammar to generate all the input strings which would take us from state k_i to state k_j in M and at the same time remove the symbol A from the top of the stack leaving whatever was below it undisturbed. $T(M)$ is then the language generated by A_1^{1n}.

We thus define $G = (N, T, P, S)$ where

$$N = \{A^{ij} | A \in V, 1 \le i, j \le n\},$$
$$S = A_1^{1n}$$

and P is constructed as follows. For each rule defining the pushdown function of M.

(a) if $p(k_i, A, a), k_i \in K, A \in V, a \in T \cup \{\varepsilon\}$ contains $(k_j, B_1 B_2 \ldots B_m)$, $k_j \in K$, $B_1, B_2, \ldots, B_m \in V$ then

$$A^{ij} \to a B_1^{i n_1} B_2^{n_1 n_2} \ldots B_m^{n_{m-1} j}$$

is in P for all $1 \le n_1, n_2, \ldots, n_{m-1} \le n$, and

(b) if $p(k_i, A, a), k_i \in K, A \in V, a \in T \cup \{\varepsilon\}$ contains $(k_j, \varepsilon), k_j \in K$, then $A^{ij} \to a$ is in P.

From the construction, it follows that $x \in T(M)$ iff $t((k_1, A_1), x)$ contains (k_n, ε) iff $A^{1n} \overset{*}{\Rightarrow} x$ iff $x \in L(G)$ and the theorem is proved.

We now have an alternative characterization of CFLs—they are the languages accepted by NPDAs. We can use this result to prove properties of the class of context-free languages.

Theorem 6.4 If L is a CFL and R is a regular set then $L \cap R$ is a CFL. *Proof* (outline) $L = T(M)$ for some NPDA $M = (K, T, V, p, k_1, A_1, F)$ and $R = T(\tilde{M})$ for some NFSA $\tilde{M} = (\tilde{K}, T, \tilde{t}, \tilde{k}_1, \tilde{F})$. We will construct an NPDA $M \times \tilde{M}$ that accepts $L \cap R$. Essentially, the NPDA $M \times \tilde{M}$ simulates the action of M and $\tilde{M}$ in parallel and if and only if x would be accepted by both automata will x be accepted by $M \times \tilde{M}$.

Formally, $M \times \tilde{M} = (K \times \tilde{K}, T, V, p', [k_1, \tilde{k}_1], A_1, F \times \tilde{F})$ where p' is defined according to the following rules: for $k, k' \in K$, $\tilde{k}, \tilde{k}' \in \tilde{K}$, $A \in V, a \in T, X \in V^*$,

(a) $([k', \tilde{k}'], X) \in p'([k, \tilde{k}], A, a)$ iff $(k', X) \in p(k, A, a)$ and $\tilde{k}' \in \tilde{t}(\tilde{k}, a)$,

(b) $[k', \tilde{k}'], X) \in p'([k, \tilde{k}], A, \varepsilon)$ iff $(k', X) \in p(k, A, \varepsilon)$ and $\tilde{k}' = \tilde{k}$.

A simple induction argument on the number of steps used in the computation shows that $t_{M \times \tilde{M}}(([k_1, \tilde{k}_1], A_1), x)$ contains $([k, \tilde{k}], X)$ iff $t_M((k_1, A_1), x)$ contains (k, X) and $\tilde{t}(\tilde{k}_1, x)$ contains $\tilde{k}$. Hence, $x \in T(M \times \tilde{M})$ iff $t_{M \times \tilde{M}}(([k_1, \tilde{k}_1], A_1), x)$ contains $([k, \tilde{k}], X)$ for some $k \in F$, $\tilde{k} \in \tilde{F}$, $X \in V^*$ iff $f_M((k_1, A_1), x)$ contains $(k, X), k \in F$, $X \in V^*$ and $\tilde{t}(\tilde{k}_1, x)$ contains $\tilde{k}, \tilde{k} \in \tilde{F}$ iff $x \in T(M)$ and $x \in T(\tilde{M})$. Thus, $T(M \times \tilde{M}) = T(M) \cap T(\tilde{M}) = L \cap R$ and the theorem is proved.

DETERMINISTIC PDAs

If the pushdown automation can make at most one move in any configuration then it is called deterministic. More formally, a pushdown automaton $M = (K, T, V, p, k_1, A_1, F)$ is a *deterministic pushdown automaton* (DPDA) if for all $k \in K$, $a \in T$, $A \in V$,

(1) $p(k, A, a)$ contains at most one element,
(2) $p(k, A, \varepsilon)$ contains at most one element, and
(3) if $p(k, A, \varepsilon) \neq \varnothing$ then $p(k, A, a) = \varnothing$ for all $a \in T$.

This third requirement ensures that if a move is possible with no input then no other move can be made from that same configuration.

The definition of a DPDA ensures that the rules defining such an automaton all have right hand sides which are either singleton sets or empty. Since, by convention, we do not explicitly state rules with empty right-hand sides, all the stated rules will be of the form

$$f(k, A, a) = \{(k', X)\}.$$

In common with most authors, we will write such rules simply as

$$f(k, A, a) = (k', X).$$

A language accepted by a DPDA is called a *deterministic context-free language* (DCFL) or often just a *deterministic language*. Unfortunately, not every CFL is deterministic but the DCFLs are nevertheless a very important class of languages. If a CFL can be accepted by a DPDA then the solution of the derivation problem is made considerably easier. The syntax definitions of most modern programming languages are designed so that programs in the language can be reasonably easily compiled. Depending upon the precise properties of the syntax definition, parsers of greater or lesser efficiency can be designed. Restricting the syntax to define a deterministic language is usually the very weakest constraint that is imposed. Further implications of this and stronger constraints will be discussed in the next two chapters. The rest of this chapter is devoted to examples and properties of deterministic languages.

Our first observation concerns the regular sets. Since every regular set can be accepted by a DFSA and since every such automaton can be easily simulated by a DPDA which makes no effective use of its stack, it follows that every regular set is deterministic. However, not every DCFL is regular as shown by the following example of DPDA which accepts the non-regular language $\{a^n b^n | n \geq 1\}$.

$M = (\{k_1, k_2, k_3\}, \{a, b\}, \{a, \dashv\}, p, k_1, \dashv, \{k_3\})$ where

$$p(k_1, \dashv, a) = (k_1, a \dashv),$$
$$p(k_1, a, a) = (k_1, aa),$$
$$p(k_1, a, b) = (k_2, \varepsilon),$$
$$p(k_2, a, b) = (k_2, \varepsilon),$$
and $\quad p(k_2, \dashv, \varepsilon) = (k_3, \varepsilon),$

Whilst in state k_1 this DPDA simply pushes each incoming a until the first b arrives, then it changes to the popping state, k_2. In this state, each incoming b is matched against a stacked a. Providing the number of pushed a's equals the number of incoming b's, the stack will eventually contain just $\dashv$ and no further input is required to enter the final state.

Clearly, every deterministic language is a CFL since it is accepted by a DPDA and this is just a restricted type of NPDA. In Exercise 5.12, we discovered that there is a CFL, $L \subset T^*$, such that its complement, $\bar{L} = T^* \backslash L$, is not a CFL. We will now show that the complement of a DCFL is necessarily a DCFL. The proof which we outline is quite complex and can be safely skipped at a first reading. The implication of the result is important, however, since it shows that there are CFLs which are not deterministic.

Let $L \subset T^*$ be a deterministic language generated by the DPDA $M = (K, T, V, p, k_1, A_1, F)$. We essentially want to interchange the rôles of final and nonfinal states thereby constructing a DPDA $\bar{M}$ which accepts $\bar{L} = T^* \backslash L$. However, there are problems that must be overcome before this approach can work.

The first difficulty is that M may have some 'dead-ends', i.e. there may be some $x \in T^*$ such that when a proper prefix of x is input to M we get a configuration either from which no move is possible or from which an infinite sequence of ε-moves can be made. In either case, $x \in \bar{L}$ and we need to construct $\bar{M}$ with care if it is to accept such strings. This is a similar type of difficulty to the one we encountered in the proof of Theorem 3.4 when we showed that the complement of a regular set is necessarily regular. As in that proof, the difficulty is overcome by a suitable modification of the original automaton. We construct from M a new DPDA, M', such that $T(M) = T(M')$ but M' always scans the whole input. M' will be the same as M except that it will be equipped with a bottom-of-stack marker $\dashv \notin V$ and three additional states $s, d, f \notin K$. M' starts in state s with $\dashv$ on the stack and immediately makes an ε-move changing to state k_1 and pushing $A_1 \dashv$ on the stack. M' then proceeds to simulate the action of M but with important modifications. Where M would have no possible move, M' moves to the dummy state, d, and there absorbs the rest of the input. The introduced state, f, is an additional final state which is used in overcoming the problem arising when M can make an infinite sequence of ε-moves. If such an infinite sequence of ε-moves is possible from some configuration, c, then there must be a configuration $c' = (k, AX), k \in K, A \in V \cup \{\dashv\}, X \in (V \cup \{\dashv\})^*$ reachable from c by a finite sequence of ε-moves such that from c' an infinite sequence of ε-moves can be made without popping any element of X. Either during this infinite sequence of moves a final state can be entered or no final state can be entered. In the first case, we define M' to ensure that configuration $c' = (k, AX)$ changes to (f, AX) given an input of ε and in the second case we define it to change to $(d, A X)$ on the same input. In order that M' still scans the whole input, we must also remember to move to d after entering f.

Formally, we define

$$M' = (K', T, V', p', s, \dashv, F')$$

where

$$K' = K \cup \{s, d, f\} \text{ is such that } s, d, f \notin K,$$
$$V' = V \cup \{\dashv\} \text{ is such that } \dashv \notin V,$$
$$F' = F \cup \{f\},$$

and p' is defined as follows:

(a) $p'(s, \dashv, \varepsilon) = (k_1, A_1 \dashv)$,

(b) for every $k \in K$, $A \in V$, $a \in T$ such that $p(k, A, a)$ and $p(k, A, \varepsilon)$ are both $\varnothing$, $p'(k, A, a) = (d, A)$,

(c) $p'(d, A, a) = (d, A)$, for all $A \in V', a \in T$,

(d) for every $k \in K, A \in V$ such that an infinite sequence of ε-moves can be made from an initial configuration (k, A),

$$p'(k, A, \varepsilon) = \begin{cases} (d, A) \text{ if none of these moves takes } M \text{ to a} \\ \qquad \text{final state,} \\ (f, A) \text{ otherwise.} \end{cases}$$

(e) $p'(f, A, \varepsilon) = (d, A)$, for all $A \in V'$,

(f) if $p'(k, A, a)$ is not defined by (a) to (d) above then $p'(k, A, a) = p(k, A, a)$, $k \in K$, $A \in V$, $a \in T \cup \{\varepsilon\}$.

The reader should be able to convince himself that $T(M) = T(M')$ and that M' will always scan the whole input. However, he may be concerned about how the construction can be achieved. In particular, in step (d), given a configuration (k, A), can we determine whether an infinite sequence of ε-moves can be made from it and if so, can we find out whether the DPDA enters a final state during such moves? The answer to both questions is 'yes'—See Exercise 6.11 at the end of this chapter.

Before we can reverse the rôles of final and nonfinal states, we still have one further problem to overcome. This arises if after an input of $x \in T^*$, M' makes several ε-moves. M' may be in final states after some of these moves and in nonfinal states after others. Reversing the role of final and nonfinal states will not alter this situation. To overcome this problem, we will have to construct yet another DFSA, M'' from M' such that $T(M'') = T(M') = T(M)$. M'' has the states of M' provided with suffices designed to remember whether or not the automaton has visited a final state since the last nonempty input. If M' has entered a final state since the last nonempty input then M'' will be in a state with suffix 1. However, if M' has not entered a final state since the last nonempty input, M'' will be in a state with suffix 2.

If M'' reads a nonempty input it will change to a state with suffix 1 or 2 depending upon whether the corresponding state of M' is or is not a final state.

Formally, if $M' = (K', T, V', p', s, \dashv, F')$, then we define $M'' = (K'', T, V', p'', s'', \dashv, F'')$ where

$$K'' = \{k_i \mid k \in K', i = 1 \text{ or } 2\},$$

$$s'' = \begin{cases} s_1 & \text{if } \varepsilon \in T(M), \\ s_2 & \text{otherwise}, \end{cases}$$

$$F'' = \{k_1 \mid k \in K'\},$$

and p'' is defined as follows:

(a) for $k \in K'$, $A \in V'$, if $p'(k, A, \varepsilon) = (k', X)$, $k' \in K'$, $X \in (V')^*$, then

$$p''(k_1, A, \varepsilon) = (k_1'', X)$$

and $p''(k_2, A, \varepsilon) = \begin{cases} (k_1', X) & \text{if } k' \in F', \\ (k_2', X) & \text{otherwise}. \end{cases}$

(b) for $k \in K'$, $A \in V'$, $a \in T$, if $p'(k, A, a) = (k', X)$, $k' \in K'$, $X \in (V')^*$, then

$$p''(k_1, A, a) = p''(k_2, A, a) = \begin{cases} (k_1', X) & \text{if } k' \in F', \\ (k_2', X) & \text{otherwise}. \end{cases}$$

We can now safely interchange the rôles of the final and nonfinal states of M'' to achieve a DPDA $\bar{M}$ which accepts $\bar{L}$. This construction yields the result.

Theorem 6.5

If $L \subset T^*$ is a deterministic language then so is $\bar{L} = T^* \backslash L$.

As a result of this and our earlier discussion, we have proved the following theorem.

Theorem 6.6

(a) Every regular language is deterministic but there are deterministic languages which are not regular;

(b) every deterministic language is context-free but there are context-free languages which are not deterministic.

The properties of deterministic languages differ considerably from those of CFLs. We have outlined a proof that deterministic languages are closed

Table 6.2 Closure properties

Closed under	Regular	Deterministic	Context-free
union	yes	no	yes
concatenation	yes	no	yes
complement	yes	yes	no
intersection	yes	no	no
Kleene closure	yes	no	yes
intersection with			
regular sets	yes	yes	yes
homomorphism	yes	no	yes

under complementation, i.e. L is deterministic implies $\bar{L}$ is deterministic, but this is not the only closure property by which the two classes of languages differ. Table 6.2 summarizes some of the known closure properties of regular sets, deterministic languages and context-free languages.

EXERCISES

1 Given an input of 012345 and a stack S, which of the following strings can be obtained as output using just PUSH and POP operations on S?
  (a) 543210,
  (b) 534210,
  (c) 431250,
  (d) 415320,
  (e) 542301.
(In general, given an input of $x = a_1 a_2 \ldots a_n$ where $a_1, \ldots, a_n$ are distinct symbols there are $n!$ distinct possible permutations. However, only $\dfrac{1}{n+1}\dbinom{2n}{n}$ are obtainable from x using a single stack with simple PUSH and POP operations. The reader is referred to *Graph Algorithms* by Shimon Even, published by Pitman Publishing Ltd, for a simple and elegant proof of this result.)

2 Construct DPDAs to show that the following are deterministic languages.
(a) $\{wcw^r \mid w \in \{a, b\}^*\}$,
(b) $\{a^i b^j \mid j > i\}$.

3 Prove that if L is deterministic and R is regular then $L \cap R$ is deterministic.

4 A NPDA, $M = (K, T, V, p, k_1, A_1, F)$ is said to *accept a language* $E(M) \subset T^*$ *by empty store* if $E(M) = \{x \mid t_M((k_1, A_1), x)$ contains (k, ε) for some $k \in K\}$. Show that $E(M)$ is necessarily context-free. (The converse is also true, i.e. for every CFL, L, there exists some NPDA, M such that $L = E(M)$. This follows from Theorem 6.2.)

5 Design an NPDA to accept the strings generated by the grammar with productions

$$S \rightarrow aA \mid aBB$$
$$A \rightarrow Ba \mid Sb$$
$$B \rightarrow bAS \mid \varepsilon$$

6 Let L be a deterministic language. Show that $MIN(L) = \{x \mid x \in L$ and no $w \in L$ is a proper prefix of $x\}$ is also deterministic.

7 Use the fact that $\{a^i b^j c^k \mid i \neq j$ and $j \neq k\}$ is not a CFL to prove that $\{a^i b^j c^k \mid i = j$ or $j = k\}$ is not deterministic. Hence, show that there exist two deterministic languages L_1, L_2 such that $L_1 \cup L_2$ is not deterministic.

8 Use the result of Exercise 6.7 to show that deterministic languages are not closed under intersection.

9 Show that every DCFL is accepted by a DPDA, M, such that no single move involves pushing more than two symbols of the stack alphabet.

10 Show that every DCFL, $L \subset T^*$, is accepted by a DPDA, $M = (K, T, V, p, k_1, A_1 . F)$ such that if a move is defined by $p(k, A, a) = (k', X), k, k' \in K, a \in T \cup \{\varepsilon\}, A \in V, X \in V^*$, then it is necessarily of one of the following types.

(a) a simple pop, i.e. $X = \varepsilon$,

(b) a push resulting in the addition of single symbol to the stack, i.e. $X = BA, A, B \in V$, or

(c) a move where the stack remains unaltered, i.e. $X = A$.

11 Consider a DPDA, $M = (\{k_1, \ldots, k_n\}, T, \{A_1, \ldots, A_m\}, p, k_1, A_1, F)$ satisfying the properties of Exercise 6.10. Define Boolean 3-dimensional arrays B_1, B_2, B_3 by

$$B_1[i, j, k] = true \text{ iff } t_M((k_i, A_k), \varepsilon) \text{ contains } (k_j, A_k),$$
$$B_2[i, j, k] = true \text{ iff } t_M((k_i, A_k), \varepsilon) \text{ contains } (k_j, \varepsilon),$$
$$B_3[i, j, k] = true \text{ iff } t_M((k_i, A_k), \varepsilon) \text{ contains } (k_j, X) \text{ for some } X \in V^*.$$

Give iterative algorithms for the construction of B_1, B_2, B_3 from M. Hence, show that step (d) in the construction of M' in the text can be effectively computed.

Chapter 7

Top-down Parsing

Iam nova progenies caelo demittitur alto
(A new generation now descends from above)
VIRGIL
Eclogues IV

In Chapter 6, we showed that NPDAs are the acceptors for CFLs. In general, the nondeterministic nature of these machines means that a parser for a CFL will involve some backtracking. The parsing algorithm proceeds deterministically and when faced with a choice of possible moves it must choose just one to develop. This means that wrong choices can sometimes be made and hence this need for backtracking. However, if certain restrictions are placed on the grammar defining a language, efficient stack-based parsing algorithms can be designed using well-known techniques. In practice, language designers are well aware of these restrictions and endeavour to design their programming language accordingly so that a compiler can be readily and efficiently produced.

There are two basic ways in which we can approach the task of parsing a string $x = a_1 a_2 \ldots a_n \in L(G)$. Firstly, we can build the derivation tree *top-down*, i.e. start with the root node, S, and develop the tree from the top in such a way that its leaf nodes are $a_1, a_2, \ldots, a_n$. Alternatively, we can attempt a *bottom-up* approach, i.e. start with x and try and deduce the internal nodes of the tree from the bottom right up to the root node, S. In Fig. 7.1, these two approaches are illustrated using the string abba\$ and the CFG, G_1, with productions

$$S \rightarrow C\$$$
$$C \rightarrow bA \,|\, aB$$
$$A \rightarrow a \,|\, aC$$
$$B \rightarrow b \,|\, bC$$

In this chapter, we will confine our attention to what is termed '*LL* parsing', which is a top-down method and leave discussion of bottom-up methods to Chapter 8. For a language to yield to an *LL* parsing technique, quite stringent restrictions have to be placed on the grammar defining it. However, in practice, although this means we can only use the technique on a subclass of the deterministic languages, these restrictions do not seem too

85

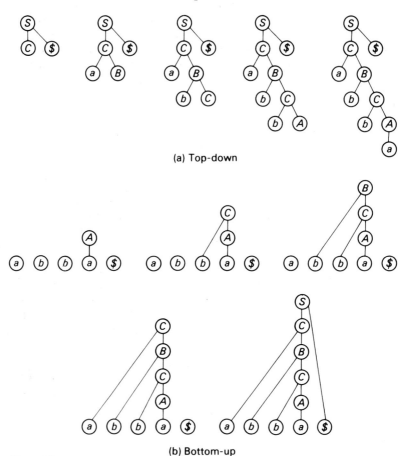

(a) Top-down

(b) Bottom-up

Figure 7.1

severe since it is one of the principle techniques used in modern-day compilers.

LL(K) GRAMMARS

Consider again the CFG, G_1. The top-down construction of the parse tree for the string *abba*$ is illustrated in Fig. 7.1a. How was this achieved? We start with the node Ⓢ and there is only one production to apply, resulting in

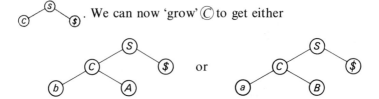

. We can now 'grow' Ⓒ to get either

or

depending upon which production, $C \to bA$ or $C \to aB$, we apply. Now, since *abba$* starts with an *a*, the second of these possibilities must be correct, i.e. by looking at the first symbol of the input, we know which production to apply. We have now generated an *a* to match the first *a* of the input string and need to check that $B \overset{*}{\Rightarrow} bba$. The node *B* can be expanded in two ways to get either

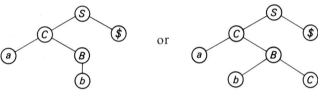

or

This time, checking the next unmatched input symbol does not tell us which of these two options to take. However, a two-symbol lookahead suffices — if the next two unmatched symbols are *b$* we must opt for the first but if they are *ba* or *bb*, we opt for the second. Knowing that in our case, the next two symbols are *bb* we opt for the second and then we need to expand *C* and check that $C \overset{*}{\Rightarrow} ba$. One symbol lookahead tells us to use the production $C \to bA$ and finally a two-symbol lookahead tells us that the final production should be $A \to a$. The construction of the derivation tree has thus corresponded to the leftmost derivation $S \Rightarrow C\$ \Rightarrow aB\$ \Rightarrow abC\$ \Rightarrow abbA\$ \Rightarrow abba\$$.

G_1 is an example of a (strong) *LL*(2) grammar, i.e. at most a two-symbol lookahead is sufficient to choose between the various productions which could be applied at any stage of a leftmost derivation. An *LL(k) grammar* $(k \geq 1)$ is one where given any sentential form $wA\gamma, w \in T^*, A \in N, \gamma \in (N \cup T)^*$, generated by a leftmost derivation, at most a *k*-symbol lookahead is required to uniquely determine which of the productions with *A* on the lefthand side should next be applied. The first *L* in *LL* stands for 'left to right scanning' and the second *L* stands for 'constructing a leftmost derivation'. Thus, with an *LL(k)* grammar, which production to apply may depend not only upon the nonterminal, *A*, to be expanded and the next *k* unmatched input symbols, but also perhaps on the string $w \in T^*$ before *A* in the sentential form and the string $\gamma \in (N \cup T)^*$ after *A* in the sentential form. If the next production to be applied can be uniquely determined from just the nonterminal to be expanded and the next *k* unmatched input symbols, the grammar is said to be *strong LL(k)*.

To define these concepts formally, we first need to define

$$\mathrm{FIRST}_k : T^* \to T^* \text{ by}$$

$$\mathrm{FIRST}_k(x) = \begin{cases} x & \text{if } |x| \leq k, \\ y & \text{if } x = yz, y \in T^k, z \in T^*. \end{cases}$$

Then, FIRST_k is extended to act on languages by defining

$$\mathrm{FIRST}_k(L) = \{\mathrm{FIRST}_k(x) | x \in L\} \text{ for all } L \subset T^*.$$

We can now give the formal definitions of $LL(k)$ and strong $LL(k)$.

Let $G = (N, T, P, S)$ be a CFG. G is said to $LL(k)$ $(k \geq 1)$ if whenever there exist two leftmost derivations,

$$S \overset{*}{\Rightarrow} wA\gamma \Rightarrow wa\gamma \overset{*}{\Rightarrow} wy \in T^*$$

and

$$S \overset{*}{\Rightarrow} wA\gamma \Rightarrow w\beta\gamma \overset{*}{\Rightarrow} wz \in T^*,$$

then $\text{FIRST}_k(y) = \text{FIRST}_k(z)$ implies $\alpha = \beta$.

G is said to be *strong* $LL(k)$ $(k \geq 1)$ if whenever there exist two leftmost derivations,

$$S \overset{*}{\Rightarrow} wA\gamma \Rightarrow wa\gamma \overset{*}{\Rightarrow} wy \in T^*$$

and

$$S \overset{*}{\Rightarrow} xA\delta \Rightarrow x\beta\delta \overset{*}{\Rightarrow} xz \in T^*,$$

then $\text{FIRST}_k(y) = \text{FIRST}_k(z)$ implies $\alpha = \beta$.

In general, it is impossible to determine whether a CFG is ambiguous or not. However, if we can show the grammar is strong $LL(k)$ then, by the following result, it must be unambiguous. In fact, this result also holds for $LL(k)$ grammars (see Exercise 7.7).

Theorem 7.1

If $G = (N, T, P, S)$ is a strong $LL(k)$ grammar $(k \geq 1)$ then G is unambiguous.
Proof Suppose G is ambiguous, i.e. there exists $w \in L(G)$ with two distinct, leftmost derivations from S. We will seek a contradiction.

Let T_1, T_2 be the derivation trees corresponding to the two distinct, leftmost derivations of $w = a_1 a_2 \ldots a_n$. Both trees have root node S and external nodes $a_1, a_2, \ldots, a_n$. However, by definition they are distinct. Consider a simultaneous tour of the nodes of the two trees done using a preorder traversal, i.e. using the recursive procedure:

visit the root;

traverse the subtrees from left to right using a preorder traversal.
Using this traversal, we must encounter nodes in T_1, T_2 which have different labels. Let the first such nodes be labelled B, C (say)—see Fig. 7.2. These are not the root nodes of T_1, T_2 since they are both labelled S. Therefore these nodes have a parent and they must be identically labelled, say with A.

The derivation tree, T_1, corresponds to a leftmost derivation

$$S \overset{*}{\Rightarrow} xA\gamma_1 \Rightarrow x\alpha B\beta_1 \gamma_1 \overset{*}{\Rightarrow} xy_1 \gamma_1 \overset{*}{\Rightarrow} xy_1 z_1 = w$$

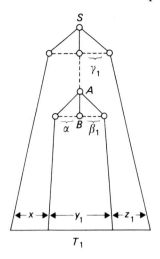
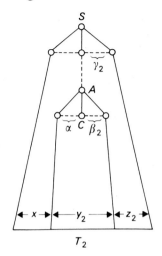

Figure 7.2

and T_2 corresponds to

$$S \overset{*}{\Rightarrow} xA\gamma_2 \Rightarrow x\alpha C\beta_2\gamma_2 \overset{*}{\Rightarrow} xy_2\gamma_2 \overset{*}{\Rightarrow} xy_2z_2 = w$$

Since $\text{FIRST}_k(y_1z_1) = \text{FIRST}_k(y_2z_2)$ and $\alpha B\beta_1 \neq \alpha C\beta_2$, it follows that G cannot be strong $LL(k)$ and the theorem is proved.

By definition, every strong $LL(k)$ grammar is $LL(k)$ but for $k > 1$, there are $LL(k)$ grammars which are not strong $LL(k)$ (see Exercise 7.5). For the case $k = 1$, however, the two definitions are equivalent (see below). It has also been shown (Rosenkrantz, D.J. & Stearns, R.E. [1970] Properties of deterministic top-down grammars. *Information and Control*, **17**, 226–256) that the class of languages generated by $LL(k)$ grammars is precisely the class of languages generated by strong $LL(k)$ grammars, for all $k \geq 1$.

Theorem 7.2

The CFG, $G = (N, T, P, S)$ is strong $LL(1)$ iff it is $LL(1)$.
Proof $\Rightarrow$: This follows immediately from the definition.
    $\Leftarrow$: Let G be an $LL(1)$ grammar that is not strong $LL(1)$. We will seek a contradiction.
    By definition, since G is not strong $LL(1)$ there exist distinct productions $A \to \alpha$, $A \to \beta$ such that for some $w, x, y_1, y_2, z_1, z_2 \in T^*$ and $\gamma, \delta \in (N \cup T)^*$,

there are two distinct leftmost derivations,

$$S \overset{*}{\Rightarrow} wA\gamma \Rightarrow w\alpha\gamma \overset{*}{\Rightarrow} wy_1\gamma \overset{*}{\Rightarrow} wy_1y_2$$

and

$$S \overset{*}{\Rightarrow} xA\delta \Rightarrow x\beta\delta \overset{*}{\Rightarrow} xz_1\delta \overset{*}{\Rightarrow} xz_1z_2,$$

where $\text{FIRST}_1(y_1y_2) = \text{FIRST}_1(z_1z_2)$.

We need to show that G is not $LL(1)$. Either (a) $y_1 = z_1 = \varepsilon$ in which case G is clearly not $LL(1)$ or (b) $y_1z_1 \neq \varepsilon$. In case (b), without loss of generality, we can assume that $y_1 \neq \varepsilon$. Hence $\text{FIRST}_1(y_1y_2) = \text{FIRST}_1(y_1) = \text{FIRST}_1(z_1z_2)$. But then the two leftmost derivations,

$$S \overset{*}{\Rightarrow} xA\delta \Rightarrow x\alpha\delta \overset{*}{\Rightarrow} xy_1\delta \Rightarrow xy_1z_2$$

and

$$S \overset{*}{\Rightarrow} xA\delta \Rightarrow x\beta\delta \overset{*}{\Rightarrow} xz_1\delta \Rightarrow xz_1z_2,$$

satisfy $\text{FIRST}_1(y_1) = \text{FIRST}_1(z_1z_2)$ but $\alpha \neq \beta$ so G is not $LL(1)$. This contradiction completes the proof of the theorem.

The special case of $LL(k)$ grammars where $k = 1$ is of particular importance in compiler writing. Language designers often endeavour to define the syntax such that, in the main, it is $LL(1)$. Even if the grammar has not been specified with this in mind, the compiler writer can sometimes transform the rules to achieve an equivalent $LL(1)$ form. One way of doing this is to use Foster's Syntax Improving Device (SID), details of which were published in the *Computer Journal* as long ago as 1968. SID automatically converts any input grammar to an equivalent $LL(1)$ form if it possibly can. However, there are usually some parts of the syntax that cannot be defined by an $LL(1)$ grammar and these have to be handled separately. Having produced an $LL(1)$ grammar for the majority of the syntax, it is easy to design or even automatically generate a parser for these rules using a technique known as recursive descent. The remaining rules are then embedded in this parser using more ad hoc techniques. This is the approach used in nearly all Pascal compilers. Recursive descent is not only applicable to $LL(1)$ grammars—it is an important technique which leads to elegant and efficient parsers for a wide variety of (deterministic) grammars. We will be discussing it in detail in the next section.

We will first develop a theorem which leads to an algorithm to test whether or not an arbitrary CFG, G, is (strong) $LL(1)$. To do this, we need to construct from G a grammar, G', such that $L(G') = \{x\$ | x \in L(G)\}$ where $\$$ is a special end-of-input marker. Thus if $G = (N, T, P, S)$ is an arbitrary CFG, we define the *augmented grammar* to be $G' = (N', T', P', S')$ where

$N' = N \cup \{S'\}$ is such that $S' \notin N$,

$T' = T \cup \{\$\}$ is such that $\$ \notin T$,

and

$P' = P \cup \{S' \to S\$\}$.

Clearly, $L(G') = \{x\$ | x \in L(G)\}$.

We now define the following functions on $N' \cup T'$.

$$\text{EMPTY}(X) = \begin{cases} true \text{ if } X \overset{*}{\Rightarrow} \varepsilon, \\ false \text{ otherwise.} \end{cases}$$

$\text{FIRST}(X) = \{a | a \in T' \text{ and } X \overset{*}{\Rightarrow} ax \text{ for some } x \in (T')^*\}$.

$\text{FOLLOW}(X) = \{a | a \in T' \text{ and } S' \overset{*}{\Rightarrow} xXay \text{ for some } x \in T^* \text{ and } y \in (T')^*\}$.

Thus with each $X \in N' \cup T'$ we associate two subsets of T', the FIRST set for X, FIRST(X), and the FOLLOW set for X, FOLLOW(X).

The function EMPTY is extended to be a function on $(N' \cup T')^*$ by defining

$\text{EMPTY}(\varepsilon) = true$, and

$\text{EMPTY}(X\alpha) = \text{EMPTY}(X) \text{ and } \text{EMPTY}(\alpha), X \in N' \cup T', \alpha \in (N' \cup T')^*$

Thus if $\gamma \in (N' \cup T')^*$, EMPTY$(\gamma)$ is *true* iff $\gamma \overset{*}{\underset{G'}{\Rightarrow}} \varepsilon$ iff $\gamma \overset{*}{\underset{G}{\Rightarrow}} \varepsilon$.

Finally, we define the function LOOKAHEAD on productions of G by

$\text{LOOKAHEAD } (A \to X_1 X_2 \ldots X_n)$
$= \bigcup \{\text{FIRST}(X_i) | 1 \le i \le n \text{ and } \text{EMPTY}(X_1 X_2 \ldots X_{i-1})\}$
$\cup \text{ if } \text{EMPTY}(X_1 X_2 \ldots X_n) \text{ then } \text{FOLLOW}(A) \text{ else } \varnothing$

The next theorem then follows from these definitions.

Theorem 7.3

The CFG, $G = (N, T, P, S)$ is (strong) $LL(1)$ iff for each pair of distinct productions $A \to \alpha$ and $A \to \beta$, in the grammar, both with the same left-hand side, $\text{LOOKAHEAD}(A \to \alpha) \cap \text{LOOKAHEAD}(A \to \beta) = \varnothing$

As an example of the use of this theorem to determine whether or not a CFG is $LL(1)$ consider the grammar $G_2 = (N, T, P, S)$ where $N = \{S, A, B\}$, $T = \{a, b, c, d\}$ and P comprises

$S \to BA | AAd$

$A \to a | \varepsilon$

$B \to bA | cB$

The corresponding augmented grammar has $N' = N \cup \{S'\} = \{S, A, B, S'\}$, $T' = T \cup \{\$\} = \{a, b, c, d, \$\}$ and p' defined by

$$S' \rightarrow S\$$$

$$S \rightarrow BA \mid AAd$$

$$A \rightarrow a \mid \varepsilon$$

$$B \rightarrow bA \mid cB$$

EMPTY(A) = *true* but EMPTY(X) = *false*, for all other $X \in N' \cup T'$. Clearly, FIRST(a_i) = $\{a_i\}$, for all $a_i \in T'$, and FOLLOW(S') = FOLLOW($\$$) = $\varnothing$ as always with an augmented grammar. Also, in such a grammar S' does not appear on the righthand side of any production, so FIRST(S') does not feature in the calculation of the LOOKAHEAD sets. We thus confine our attention to the calculation of FIRST(A_i), $A_i \in N$ and FOLLOW(X), $X \in N \cup T$.

The values FIRST(A_i), $A_i \in N$, can be expressed as the solution of a set of equations constructed according to the following rule.

$$\text{FIRST}(A_i) = \bigcup \{\text{FIRST}(X_{ij}) | \text{there is a production } A_i \rightarrow$$
$$X_{i1} X_{i2} \ldots X_{in} \text{ and either } j = 1 \text{ or EMPTY}$$
$$(X_{i1} X_{i2} \ldots X_{ij-1})\}.$$

Using this rule on our example, we deduce that

$$\text{FIRST}(S) = \text{FIRST}(B) \cup \text{FIRST}(A) \cup \text{FIRST}(A) \cup \{d\}$$
$$= \text{FIRST}(B) \cup \text{FIRST}(A) \cup \{d\}$$

$$\text{FIRST}(A) = \text{FIRST}(a) = \{a\},$$

and

$$\text{FIRST}(B) = \text{FIRST}(b) \cup \text{FIRST}(c) = \{b, c\}.$$

In general, the set of equations can be solved using the iterative technique described at the end of Chapter 5. For our example, the solution is obvious and we get the FIRST sets as tabulated in Fig. 7.3.

The FOLLOW sets can be similarly expressed as a solution to a set of equations. If $X \in N \cup T$, then

$$\text{FOLLOW}(X) = \bigcup \{\text{FOLLOW}(A_i) | \text{there is a production of form}$$
$$A_i \rightarrow \alpha X \beta \text{ and EMPTY}(\beta)\} \cup$$
$$\bigcup \{\text{FIRST}(X_{ij}) | \text{there is a production}$$
$$A_i \rightarrow \alpha X X_{i1} X_{i2} \ldots X_{in} \text{ and } j = 1$$
$$or \text{ EMPTY}(X_{i1} X_{i2} \ldots X_{ij-1})\}.$$

Table 7.1

Elements in $N' \cup T'$	FIRST SET	FOLLOW SET
\$	$\{\$\}$	$\varnothing$
a	$\{a\}$	$\{a, d, \$\}$
b	$\{b\}$	$\{a, d, \$\}$
c	$\{c\}$	$\{b, c\}$
d	$\{d\}$	$\{\$\}$
S'	$\{a, b, c, d\}^{1}$	$\varnothing$
S	$\{a, b, c, d\}$	$\{\$\}$
A	$\{a\}$	$\{a, d, \$\}$
B	$\{b, c\}$	$\{a, d, \$\}$

[1] This result is not needed but is included for completeness sake.
FIRST(S') = FIRST$(S) \cup$ *if* EMPTY(S) *then* $\{\$\}$ *else* $\varnothing$.

Hence, for our example we deduce that

$$\text{FOLLOW}(a) = \text{FOLLOW}(A)$$
$$\begin{aligned}\text{FOLLOW}(b) &= \text{FOLLOW}(B) \cup \text{FIRST}(A)\\ &= \text{FOLLOW}(B) \cup \{a\}\end{aligned}$$
$$\text{FOLLOW}(c) = \text{FIRST}(B) = \{b, c\}$$
$$\text{FOLLOW}(d) = \text{FOLLOW}(S)$$
$$\text{FOLLOW}(S) = \text{FIRST}(\$) = \{\$\}$$

$$\begin{aligned}\text{FOLLOW}(A) &= \text{FOLLOW}(S) \cup \text{FOLLOW}(B)\\ &\quad \cup \text{FIRST}(A) \cup \text{FIRST}(d)\\ &= \text{FOLLOW}(S) \cup \text{FOLLOW}(B) \cup \{a, d\}\end{aligned}$$

$$\begin{aligned}\text{FOLLOW}(B) &= \text{FOLLOW}(S) \cup \text{FOLLOW}(B) \cup \text{FIRST}(A)\\ &= \text{FOLLOW}(S) \cup \text{FOLLOW}(B) \cup \{a\}\end{aligned}$$

Once again, these equations can be solved using the technique of Chapter 5 and the results are tabulated in Table 7.1

Having computed the FIRST and FOLLOW sets for each element in $N \cup T$, we can now compute the LOOKAHEAD sets for each production in the grammar. These are tabulated in Table 7.2. Since LOOKAHEAD $(A \rightarrow a) \cap$ LOOKAHEAD$(A \rightarrow \varepsilon) \neq \varnothing$, the grammar is not $LL(1)$.

The above algorithm shows that it is possible to test whether an arbitrary CFG is $LL(1)$ or not. Unfortunately, there can be no algorithm which, given an arbitrary CFG, reports whether or not there exists an equivalent $LL(1)$ grammar—this is an unsolvable problem. Thus, if SID fails to convert an arbitrary CFG into an equivalent $LL(1)$ form, it cannot necessarily be inferred that no such grammar exists.

Table 7.2

Productions	LOOKAHEAD set
$S \to BA$	$\{b, c\}$
$S \to AAd$	$\{a, d\}$
$A \to a$	$\{a\}$
$A \to \varepsilon$	$\{a, d, \$\}$
$B \to bA$	$\{b\}$
$B \to cB$	$\{c\}$

RECURSIVE DESCENT

If G is an $LL(k)$ grammar, then it is possible to write a parser for $L(G)$ using the method known as recursive descent. Although this parsing technique does not use a stack explicitly, recursive descent does use one implicitly since it uses recursive procedures which are, of course, implemented using a stack. Thus although this technique might appear to differ from that described in Chapter 6, it is essentially similar.

In its simplest form, recursive descent provides us with a way of constructing a recognizer for the language generated by an $LL(1)$ grammar $G = (N, T, P, S)$. In such a recognizer, there is one procedure for each symbol in $N \cup T$ that is designed to recognize any string derivable from that symbol. Say $X \in N \cup T$ then we will call this procedure pX. If $a \in T$, pa simply reads the next unmatched input symbol and checks that it equals a. If $A \in N$, and the productions in P with A on the left-hand side are $A \to \alpha_1$, $A \to \alpha_2 ..., A \to \alpha_n$, then, by inspecting the next symbol to be matched and comparing this with the LOOKAHEAD sets for these productions, we can determine which production should be applied in the next step of the derivation. Thus, in the procedure, pA, depending upon the next unmatched symbol, we select a production $A \to \alpha_i$ (say) to be used next. If $\alpha_i = X_{i1} X_{i2} ... X_{im}$, $X_{ij} \in N \cup T$, $1 \le j \le m$, then we simply call pX_{i1}; $pX_{i2}, ...; pX_{im}$.

As an example, consider the following grammar, G_3, which is clearly $LL(1)$

Table 7.3

Production	LOOKAHEAD sets
$S \to aAB$	$\{a\}$
$S \to bS$	$\{b\}$
$A \to aA$	$\{a\}$
$A \to bB$	$\{b\}$
$B \to AB$	$\{a, b\}$
$B \to c$	$\{c\}$

$$S \to aAB|bS$$
$$A \to aA|bB$$
$$B \to AB|c$$

with LOOKAHEAD sets as tabulated in Table 7.3.

We will assume that *nextsymbol* is a function which allows us to 'peep' at the next unmatched input symbol without actually removing it from the input stream. A simple recursive descent recognizer for $L(G_3)$ written in a Pascal-like code is.

```
begin pS; if no more input then halt else fail end
where
procedure pS ≡ case nextsymbol of
                'a': pa; pA; pB;
                'b': pb; pS;
                'c': fail
                end;
procedure pA ≡ case nextsymbol of
                'a': pa; pA;
                'b': pb; pB;
                'c': fail
                end;
procedure pB ≡ case nextsymbol of
                'a', 'b': pA; pB;
                'c': pc
                end;
procedure pa ≡ begin
                read(symbol); if symbol ≠ 'a' then fail
                end;
procedure pb ≡ begin
                read(symbol); if symbol ≠ 'b' then fail
                end;
procedure pc ≡ begin
                read(symbol); if symbol ≠ 'c' then fail
                end;
```

and fail is a procedure which aborts the process and reports accordingly.

The next step is the insertion of *semantic actions* into the procedures of the recognizer, i.e. the insertion of code to ensure that some internal representation of a valid input is delivered as a result. If this internal representation is a derivation tree then we will have an algorithm to solve the derivation problem. In practice, compiler writers insert code to deliver a more appropriate internal form such as the semantic trees we described in Chapter 2. We will illustrate this by using the grammar which generates arithmetic expressions over the variables a, b, c terminated by an end-of-input marker,

$$S \rightarrow E\$$$
$$E \rightarrow T \mid E + T \mid E - T$$
$$T \rightarrow F \mid T \times F \mid T/F$$
$$F \rightarrow a \mid b \mid c \mid (E)$$

Now, this grammar is clearly not $LL(1)$—in fact it is not $LL(k)$ for any k. This follows since for any k, E can generate $(((\ldots(a)\ldots))) + a$ and $(((\ldots(a)\ldots))) - a$ with $k + 1$ opening parentheses. A k-lookahead will not suffice to determine whether the production to be applied should be $E \rightarrow E + T$ or $E \rightarrow E - T$.

However, we should not despair. There are various approaches open to us. One obvious approach is to try and find an equivalent grammar which is $LL(1)$. The left recursion in the grammar must certainly be removed if this is to be achieved (see Exercise 7.2). Using Theorem 5.6, we construct the equivalent grammar

$$S \rightarrow E\$$$
$$E \rightarrow TA$$
$$A \rightarrow \varepsilon \mid + TA \mid - TA$$
$$T \rightarrow FB$$
$$B \rightarrow \varepsilon \mid \times FB \mid /FB$$
$$F \rightarrow a \mid b \mid c \mid (E)$$

Now, this grammar is $LL(1)$ and hence we can easily design a recursive descent recognizer from it. Unfortunately, the insertion of the semantic

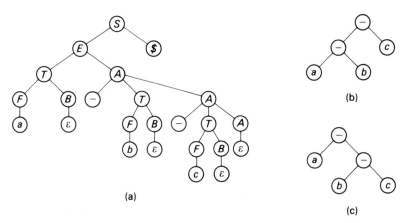

(a)

(b)

(c)

Figure 7.3

actions, although possible, is then quite tricky. Our original grammar had been carefully designed so that the correct semantic tree could be easily inferred from the derivation tree. By rewriting the grammar, we have lost to some extent this desirable feature. For example, $a - b - c\$$ has the corresponding derivation tree given in Fig. 7.3a and the correct semantic tree is that of Fig. 7.3b not that of Fig. 7.3c.

An alternative approach is to represent the grammar using the syntax charts of Fig. 7.4. This avoids the use of introduced nonterminals, $A, B,$ and enables us to write a recursive descent recognizer in which the correct semantic actions can be easily inserted. With each of the nonterminals used in the syntax chart we associate a procedure. Thus we have procedures pE, pT and pF. As is usually done in practice, rather than write procedures, $p+$, $p-$ etc., for recognizing terminal symbols, we will embed the code for these in pE, pT and pF as and where necessary.

The recognizer will thus be of the following form.

begin pE; if nextsymbol = '$\$$' *then* halt *else* fail *end*
where
procedure pE ≡ begin
        pT;
        while nextsymbol = ' *+* ' *or nextsymbol =* ' *−* ' *do*
            begin
              read(symbol); *pT*
            end
      end;
procedure pT ≡ begin
        pF;
        while nextsymbol = ' *×* ' *or nextsymbol =* '*/*' *do*
            begin
              read(symbol); *pF*
            end
      end;
procedure pF ≡ begin
        case nextsymbol of
        '*a*', '*b*', '*c*': read(symbol);
        '*(*': read(symbol); *pE*; read(symbol);
           if symbol ≠ '*)*' *then* fail;
        '*)*', '$\$$': fail
      end

The next stage is the insertion of semantic actions into these procedures. There will then be a function, fX, constructed from each procedure, pX, which will deliver a semantic tree representing the arithmetic expression

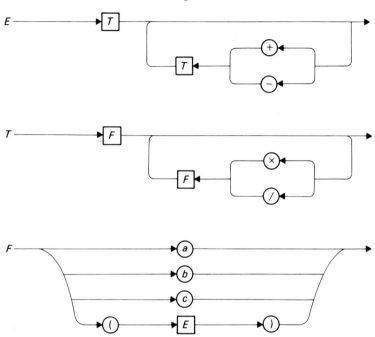

Figure 7.4

recognized by *pX*. We will assume that we have a function *tree construct* which takes three arguments, a symbol, *s*, and two trees, T_1 and T_2 in that order and constructs the tree with root labelled, *s*, left subtree, T_1, and right subtree, T_2. The empty tree is denoted by nil.

    Insertion of the semantic actions then results in the following code.

begin var t: tree; *t*: = *f E*; *if nextsymbol* = '*$*' *then t else* fail *end*
where
function f E: tree ≡ begin
                     var t: tree;
                     t: = *f T*;
                     while nextsymbol = ' + ' *or nextsymbol* = ' − ' *do*
                         begin
                           read(symbol): *t*: = *tree construct*(symbol, *t*, *f T*)
                       end;
                   f E: = *t*
                 end;
function f T:tree ≡ *begin*
                     var t:tree;
                     t: = *f F*;

```
while nextsymbol = ' × ' or nextsymbol = '/' do
    begin
        read(symbol); t: = tree construct(symbol, t, f F)
    end;
    f T: = t
end;
function f F : tree ≡ begin
    case nextsymbol of
    'a', 'b', 'c': read(symbol);
                f F: = tree construct(symbol, nil, nil);
    '(': read(symbol); f F: = f E; read(symbol);
        if symbol ≠ ')' then fail;
    ')', '$': fail
    end
```

Recursive descent has proved a most effective technique in compiler writing. We have shown that if a grammar is $LL(1)$ then a recognizer can be simply designed from the LOOKAHEAD sets. From this recognizer the semantic actions can be inserted to achieve the desired parser. In practice, however, the syntax of most programming languages cannot be fully specified using an $LL(1)$ grammar. The compiler writer may be able to use the above approach for a large percentage of the rules but there will be some rules for which it is not appropriate. This is either because these rules cannot be written in an equivalent $LL(1)$ form or because if they are so written, the insertion of semantic actions into the generated code is made unnecessarily difficult. Thus, for these rules the compiler writer must use an alternative approach. Recursive descent can still be his solution as we have seen with the arithmetic expressions example. Also, if a k-lookahead is allowed, the whole approach can obviously be generalized to cope with any $LL(k)$ grammar. For a detailed and practical application of the use of recursive descent in writing a compiler for an Algol-like language (called S-Algol), the reader is referred to *Recursive Descent Compiling* by A.J.T. Davie and R. Morrison, published by Ellis Horwood, 1981.

A more complete theoretical approach to $LL(k)$ grammars and recursive descent together with some interesting work on error recovery can be found in *Syntax of Programming Languages: Theory and Practice* by R.C. Backhouse, published by Prentice–Hall International, 1979.

EXERCISES

1 Which of the following are $LL(1)$ grammars? For each such grammar, design a corresponding recursive descent recognizer.

(a) $S \rightarrow A | B$

$A \rightarrow aA|a$

$B \rightarrow bB|b$

(b) $S \rightarrow AB$

$A \rightarrow Ba|\varepsilon$

$B \rightarrow Cb|C$

$C \rightarrow c|\varepsilon$

(c) $S \rightarrow aAaB|bAbB$

$A \rightarrow S|cb$

$B \rightarrow cB|a$

2 Remembering that by convention there are no irrelevant productions in our CFGs, show that an $LL(1)$ grammar cannot have any left-recursive productions. Is this true for $LL(k)$ grammars?

3 Generalize Theorem 7.3 and the preceding definitions to produce a necessary and sufficient condition for a grammar to be strong $LL(k)$ expressed in terms of k-LOOKAHEAD sets.

4 Using your answer to Exercise 7.3, show that the following grammar is strong $LL(2)$ and hence design a corresponding recursive descent recognizer.

$S \rightarrow aAS|AbSc|\varepsilon$

$A \rightarrow cbA|a$

5 (a) Show that the following grammar is $LL(2)$ but not strong $LL(2)$.

$S \rightarrow aAaa|bAba$

$A \rightarrow b|\varepsilon$

(b) Show that the following grammar is $LL(3)$ but not strong $LL(k)$ for any $k \geq 1$.

$S \rightarrow aBA|bBbA$

$A \rightarrow abA|c$

$B \rightarrow a|ab$

6 Show that if L is a regular language and $\$ \notin L$ then $L\$ = \{x\$|x \in L\}$ can be generated by a (strong) $LL(1)$ grammar. (Hint: work from the DFSA accepting the language L.)

7 Show that if a grammar, $G = (N, T, P, S)$, is ambiguous then there exist $w, x \in T^*, A \in N, \gamma \in (N \cup T)^*$ such that $S \overset{*}{\Rightarrow} wAy$ is a leftmost derivation and there exist two distinct derivations, $A \Rightarrow \alpha \overset{*}{\Rightarrow} x$ and $A \Rightarrow \beta \overset{*}{\Rightarrow} x$, where $\alpha, \beta \in (N \cup T)^*$ and $\alpha \neq \beta$. Use this result to show that every $LL(k)$ grammar is unambiguous.

8   Show that the grammar with productions

$$S \rightarrow C\$$$
$$C \rightarrow bA \mid aB$$
$$A \rightarrow a \mid aC \mid bAA$$
$$B \rightarrow b \mid bC \mid aBB$$

is not $LL(k)$ for any k. Can you construct an equivalent grammar which is $LL(k)$ for some k?

Chapter 8

Bottom-up Parsing

Build from the bottom up not from the top down.

FRANKLIN D. ROOSEVELT
Radio Address, 7 *April* 1932

Given an unambiguous CFG, G, and a string $x \in L(G)$, both the top-down and the bottom-up parsing techniques (if applicable) must yield the same derivation tree. The distinction between the methods lies in the way the trees are constructed. Whereas the top-down parsing techniques of Chapter 7 attempt to develop the parse tree from the top, the bottom-up method starts with the leaf nodes and works towards the root. The input string is initially scanned from left to right to find substrings which match the symbols on the right of some production rule. Once one of these substrings is found, it can be replaced by or *reduced* to the nonterminal on the left of the production rule to obtain a sentential form of the grammar. Now, working with this sentential form we again seek a substring which can be reduced. The objective is to find a sequence of these reductions which will enable us to construct the whole derivation tree starting from the bottom and building upwards until the root symbol is reached. Every reduction corresponds to the construction of yet another parent in the derivation tree.

Consider the grammar, G_1, with productions

$$S \to C\$$$
$$C \to aBC \,|\, aB \,|\, bAC \,|\, bA$$
$$A \to bAA \,|\, a$$
$$B \to aBB \,|\, b$$

From Exercise 2.5, we know that this grammar is unambiguous and thus, any $x \in L(G_1)$ has a unique derivation tree. For example, the derivation tree for $x = bbaa\$$ is given in Fig. 8.1e. Now, to every derivation tree there corresponds a unique *rightmost derivation*, i.e. a derivation in which it is the rightmost nonterminal that is always expanded. Corresponding to the example derivation tree, we have the rightmost derivation, $S \Rightarrow C\$ \Rightarrow bA\$$ $bbAA\$ \Rightarrow bbAa\$ \Rightarrow bbaa\$$. The bottom-up parsing techniques we consider will construct such a rightmost derivation but in reverse. For example, the construction of the derivation tree for $bbaa\$$ proceeds as in Fig. 8.1.

The substring which is reduced at each stage is called the *handle* of the

102

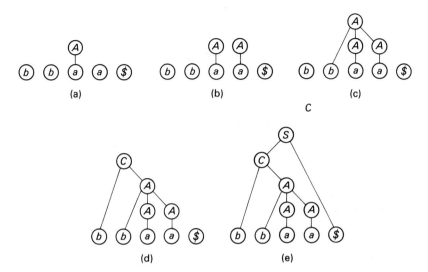

Figure 8.1

rightmost sentential form. Thus, for our example, the process can be tabulated as follows.

Rightmost Sentential form	Handle	Replaced by
bbaa$	(first) *a*	*A*
bbAa$	*a*	*A*
bbAA$	*bAA*	*A*
bA$	*bA*	*C*
C$	*C$*	*S*

The central problem with the bottom-up technique is to find and suitably reduce the handle at each step.

SIMPLE PRECEDENCE GRAMMARS

We will first solve the problem of finding and reducing the handle for a small class of grammars called simple precedence grammars.

We will scan the rightmost sentential form from left to right looking at pairs of adjacent symbols trying to locate the handle's tail, i.e. its rightmost symbol. Once this is located, we move leftwards from the tail to locate the handle's head, i.e. its leftmost symbol.

Let $G = (N, T, P, S)$ be a CFG and let $\alpha X Y \beta$ be a rightmost sentential form, α, $\beta \in (N \cup T)^*$, X, $Y \in N \cup T$. At some point in the reduction of this sentential form to S, one of the three following possibilities arise:

(a) X is part of the handle but Y is not. Thus X is the tail of the handle. In this case, we say X has precedence over Y and write $X \gtrdot Y$.

(b) X and Y are both in the handle. We then say X and Y have equal precedence and write $X \doteq Y$.

(c) Y is part of the handle but X is not. Thus Y is the head of the handle and we say it has precedence over X, written $X \lessdot Y$.

The relations $\gtrdot$, $\doteq$ and $\lessdot$ are called *simple precedence relations*. It follows from these definitions that

(a) $X \gtrdot Y$ iff Y is a terminal symbol (remember that $\alpha X Y \beta$ is a sentential form in a rightmost derivation) and there exists some production $A \to \gamma_1 B Z \gamma_2$, A, $B \in N$, $Z \in N \cup T$, γ_1, $\gamma_2 \in (N \cup T)^*$ such that $B \overset{+}{\Rightarrow} \delta_1 X$ and $Z \overset{*}{\Rightarrow} Y \delta_2$, δ_1, $\delta_2 \in (N \cup T)^*$.

(b) $X \doteq Y$ iff there exists some production $A \to \gamma_1 X Y \gamma_2$, $A \in N$, γ_1, $\gamma_2 \in (N \cup T)^*$.

(c) $X \lessdot Y$ iff there exists some production $A \to \gamma_1 X B \gamma_2$, $B \in N$, γ_1, $\gamma_2 \in (N \cup T)^*$ such that $B \overset{+}{\Rightarrow} Y \delta$, $\delta \in (N \cup T)^*$.

A CFG, $G = (N, T, P, S)$, is called a *simple precedence grammar* provided: (i) no two rules of the grammar have identical right parts, and (ii) there is at most one simple precedence relation between any pair of symbols in $(N \cup T) \times (N \cup T)$.

Although G_1 satisfies the first of these conditions, it does not satisfy the second since both $a \gtrdot a$ (from $A \to bAA$, $A \overset{+}{\Rightarrow} a$ and $A \overset{*}{\Rightarrow} a$) and $a \lessdot a$ (from $C \to aB$ and $B \overset{+}{\Rightarrow} aBB$).

Now, consider the simple precedence grammar, G_2, with productions

$$S \to (R \mid a$$
$$R \to Sa)$$

The reader should verify that the simple precedence relations are those tabulated in Table 8.1.

If a grammar, $G = (N, T, P, S)$ is a simple precedence grammar, then the

Table 8.1

	S	R	a	(	)
S	.	.	$\doteq$	.	.
R	.	.	$\gtrdot$	.	.
a	.	.	$\gtrdot$	.	$\doteq$
(	$\lessdot$	$\doteq$	$\lessdot$	$\lessdot$	.
)	.	.	$\gtrdot$	.	.

handle of any rightmost sentential form can easily be found. We simply scan the sentential form for the leftmost pair of symbols X_j and X_{j+1} such that $X_j > X_{j+1} \cdot X_j$ is then the tail of the handle. Now, scan the sentential form from right to left starting at X_j until we find a pair X_{i-1}, X_i such that $X_{i-1} < X_i \cdot X_i$ is the head of the handle. Having found the handle, $\beta = X_i \ldots X_j$, there must be a unique production of the form $A \to \beta$ and so the handle β can be reduced to A. The only problem with this approach is the case where the tail of the handle is the last symbol or the head of the handle is the first. To overcome this problem, we introduce an end-marker, $\$ \notin N \cup T$, to be used at both ends of our sentential forms. We then set $\$ > X$ and $X > \$$ for all $X \in N \cup T$ and by repeated reduction of handles, the input string $\$x\$$, $x \in L(G)$ is reduced to $\$S\$$.

Now, $L(G_2)$ includes strings of the form a, (aa), $((aa)\,a)$, $(((aa)\,a)\,a)$, etc. A parse of $\$(((aa)\,a)\,a)\$$ showing the use of the precedence relations is illustrated in Table 8.2. This corresponds to a rightmost derivations $S \Rightarrow (R \Rightarrow (Sa) \Rightarrow ((Ra) \Rightarrow ((Sa)\,a) \Rightarrow (((Ra)\,a) \Rightarrow (((Sa)\,a)\,a) \Rightarrow (((aa)\,a)\,a)$.

A convenient way to implement the reduction of the handles is to use a stack and an input buffer. The primary operations will be a *push* (or *shift*) action, i.e. the next input symbol is pushed onto the top of the stack and a *reduce* action, i.e. the parser knows the handle is at the top of the stack and replaces it accordingly. The parser will accept the input if it terminates with $\$S$ on the stack and $\$$ in the buffer. At any stage, it will enter some error recovery routine if it finds no other action is possible. Parsers that are implemented in this way are sometimes known as *shift-reduce* parsers. The

Table 8.2

Sentential form	Handle
$\$$ (((a $a)a$ $)a)$ $\$$	a
$<$ $<$ $<$ $<$ $>$	
$\$$ (((S a) $a)a)\$$	$Sa)$
$<$ $<$ $<$ $<$ $=$ $=$ $>$	
$\$$ (((R $a)a$ $)\$$	$(R$
$<$ $<$ $<$ $\doteq$ $>$	
$\$$ ((S a) $a)\$$	$Sa)$
$<$ $<$ $<$ $=$ $=$ $>$	
$\$$ ((R $a)\$$	$(R$
$<$ $<$ $\doteq$ $>$)	
$\$$ (S a $\$$	$Sa)$
$<$ $<$ $\doteq$ $\doteq$ $>$	
$\$$ (R $\$$	$(R$
$<$ $\doteq$ $>$	
$\$$ S $\$$	

contents of the stack and the input buffer at each step of our example is given in Table 8.3.

It is clear that in the implementation of a shift-reduce parser for a simple precedence grammar, the shift operation is done next provided the last symbol pushed has less than or equal precedence to the next symbol in the input buffer. Where this is not the case, the symbols in the stack are popped to find the handle so that a reduce action can be taken. If no handle is found, there is an error situation.

One of the first steps in the implementation of a parser using the simple precedence parsing technique is the construction of the precedence relations and, fortunately, there is an easy algorithm to compute these (see Exercise 8.1). Storage may be a problem however if care is not taken. If the grammar has m terminal and n nonterminal symbols then there are $(m + n)^2$ possible relations. If we use a (precedence) matrix, many of the values will be $\cdot$, representing the absence of a relation. We can either store this matrix compactly using any of a variety of techniques for sparse arrays or we may be able to overcome the problem using *precedence functions*. From a precedence matrix, P, we try to construct two integer functions, f, g, such that

$$f(i) < g(j) \text{ if } P_{ij} \equiv \lessdot,$$
$$f(i) = g(j) \text{ if } P_{ij} \equiv \doteq$$

Table 8.3

Stack	Input buffer	Action
$	$(((aa)a)a)$ $	shift
$(	$((aa)a)a)$ $	shift
$((	$(aa)a)a)$ $	shift
$(((	$aa)a)a)$ $	shift
$(((a	$a)a)a)$ $	reduce using $S \to a$
$(((S	$a)a)a)$ $	shift
$(((Sa	$)a)a)$ $	shift
$(((Sa)	$a)a)$ $	reduce using $R \to Sa)$
$(((R	$a)a)$ $	reduce using $S \to (R$
$((S	$a)a)$ $	shift
$((Sa	$)a)$ $	shift
$((Sa)	$a)$ $	reduce using $R \to Sa)$
$((R	$a)$ $	reduce using $S \to (R$
$(S	$a)$ $	shift
$(Sa	$)$ $	shift
$(Sa)	$ $	reduce using $R \to Sa)$
$(R	$ $	reduce using $S \to (R$
$S	$ $	accept

and

$$f(i) > g(j) \text{ if } P_{ij} \equiv > .$$

If we can find such functions they are called precedence functions and can be stored using only $2(m + n)$ storage locations instead of $(m + n)^2$ for the corresponding precedence matrix. Some information is lost however—the absence of a precedence relation, which may be used in the detection and repair of input errors, is no longer represented.

The most serious criticism of the whole method, however, is that few grammars are simple precedence grammars and thus the technique can only be applied to just a small subclass of the CFGs.

LR(0) GRAMMARS

The bottom-up parsing method which is most widely used in practical compilers is the *LR* technique which was initially developed by Knuth (Knuth, D.E. (1965) On the translation of languages from left to right. *Information and Control*, **8**, 607–639). The *L* in *LR* stands for 'left-to-right scanning, and the *R* for 'constructing a rightmost derivation in reverse'. As with the simple precedence technique, *LR* can be viewed as a shift-reduce parser. However, the *LR* technique is much more attractive than the simple precedence technique because of its wide application. In fact, *LR* is also superior to *LL*, being suitable for a much wider class of grammars. One criticism of the method is that, unlike *LL*, it is not intuitively appealing and can be quite difficult to understand. Fortunately, the core of the algorithm can be automated and this is largely the reason for its successful use in practical situations.

With a shift-reduce parser, such as that described in Table 8.3, at any stage we have a stack contents, $\alpha \in (N \cup T)^*$, and an input buffer contents, $z \in T^*$ such that together, αz, comprises a rightmost sentential form. At each step of the parser, we can either perform another shift operation, i.e. push another symbol from the input buffer onto the stack, or we can use a reduction operation. The problem is to determine which of these to do and if it is to be a reduction operation, which production should be used. We want to impose conditions on the grammar which will ensure that from our knowledge of the stack contents, we will always know exactly what move our shift-reduce parser should make in order to construct the reverse of a rightmost derivation.

Say we have a production $A \to \beta$ and the stack contents is $\alpha = \gamma\beta$, then we can make a reduction. This must be the only move possible, i.e. it must not be possible to perform zero or more shift operations to set the stack contents to αx, $x \in T^*$ and then apply some other reduction $B \to \beta'$ (say) still achieving a rightmost sentential form. Thus we require that if there are two rightmost derivations

$$S \stackrel{*}{\Rightarrow} \gamma A x y \Rightarrow \gamma \beta x y$$

and

$$S \stackrel{*}{\Rightarrow} \delta B y \Rightarrow \delta \beta' y = \gamma \beta x y$$

where $\gamma, \delta, \beta, \beta' \in (N \cup T)^*$, $A, B \in N$ and $x, y \in T^*$ then these two derivations are the same, i.e. $\delta = \gamma, A = B, \beta = \beta'$ and $x = \varepsilon$.

The set of strings which can appear on the stack prior to a reduction using a production $A \to \beta$ is called the LRCONTEXT set of $A \to \beta$, denoted by LRCONTEXT $(A \to \beta)$. Formally,

$$\text{LRCONTEXT} (A \to \beta) = \{\alpha \mid \alpha = \gamma \beta \in (N \cup T)^*$$

where $S \stackrel{*}{\Rightarrow} \gamma A x \Rightarrow \gamma \beta x$ is a rightmost derivation, $x \in T^*$, $\gamma \in (N \cup T)^*\}$. The above condition is not satisfied if there exist distinct productions $A \to \beta$, $B \to \beta'$ such that LRCONTEXT $(A \to \beta)$ contains $\gamma \beta$ and LRCONTEXT $(B \to \beta')$ contains $\delta \beta'$ where $\delta \beta' = \gamma \beta x$ for some $x \in T^*$.

Even if a grammar meets these conditions there may be problems about when to accept and halt. For example, consider

$$S \to Sa \mid a$$

LRCONTEXT $(S \to a) = \{a\}$ and LRCONTEXT $(S \to Sa) = \{Sa\}$ so it satisfies the above conditions. However, if S is the only symbol on the stack, the parse might have finished. We do not know whether to accept and halt or perform a shift. This is not a serious problem if we allow an end-of-input marker and use the augmented grammar

$$S' \to S\$$$

$$S \to Sa \mid a.$$

Then LRCONTEXT$(S' \to S\$) = \{S\$\}$, LRCONTEXT$(S \to Sa) = \{Sa\}$ and LRCONTEXT$(S \to a) = \{a\}$.

From the above discussion, we formulate the following definition: A CFG, $G = (N, T, P, S)$ is an $LR(0)$ *grammar* if
(a) its start symbol does not appear on the right-hand side of any production, and
(b) if there are two rightmost derivations,

$$S \stackrel{*}{\Rightarrow} \gamma A x y \Rightarrow \gamma \beta x y$$

and

$$S \stackrel{*}{\Rightarrow} \delta B y \Rightarrow \delta \beta' y = \gamma \beta x y$$

where $\gamma, \delta, \beta, \beta' \in (N \cup T)^*$, $A, B \in N$ and $x, y \in T^*$ then $\delta = \gamma, A = B, \beta = \beta'$ and $x = \varepsilon$.

We also have the following theorem which results from this definition.

Theorem 8.1

A CFG, $G = (N, T, P, S)$, is an $LR(0)$ grammar iff (a) its start symbol does not appear on the right-hand side of any production and (b) if $\alpha \in \text{LRCONTEXT}(A \to \beta')$ and $\alpha x \in \text{LRCONTEXT}(B \to \beta')$ where $A \to \beta$, $B \to \beta' \in P$, $\alpha \in (N \cup T)^*$ and $x \in T^*$, then $x = \varepsilon$, $A = B$ and $\beta = \beta'$.

To check if a CFG satisfying the first condition of this theorem is an $LR(0)$ grammar, we need to calculate the LRCONTEXT sets. Now, every string in LRCONTEXT$(A \to \beta)$ is of the form $\gamma\beta$ for some $\gamma \in (N \cup T)^*$. Hence, if we define for all $A \in N$, $\text{LEFT}(A) = \{\gamma \mid S \overset{*}{\Rightarrow} \gamma A x$ is a rightmost derivation, $x \in T^*\}$, the following theorem arises.

Theorem 8.2

$$\text{LRCONTEXT}(A \to \beta) = \text{LEFT}(A) \cdot \{\beta\}.$$

Thus to find the LRCONTEXT sets of the productions of the grammar we need first to find the LEFT sets of the nonterminals. Assuming the grammar $G = (N, T, P, S)$ does not have S appearing on the right-hand side of any production, it follows that $\text{LEFT}(S) = \{\varepsilon\}$. Also, if $B \to \gamma_1 A \gamma_2$ is a production of G then $\text{LEFT}(A)$ contains $\text{LEFT}(B) \cdot \{\gamma_1\}$.

As an example of how these facts can be used to calculate LRCONTEXT sets for a grammar, consider the grammar, G_3, with productions

$$S \to A\$$$
$$A \to AB \mid B$$
$$B \to [A] \mid []$$

This grammar generates strings of balanced brackets with an end-marker $\$$, such as $[]\$$, $[[]]\$$, $[][]\$$, ...

Applying our reasoning about LEFT sets, we get the following equations

$$\text{LEFT}(S) = \{\varepsilon\}$$
$$\text{LEFT}(A) = \text{LEFT}(S) \cup \text{LEFT}(A) \cup \text{LEFT}(B) \cdot \{[\}$$
$$\text{LEFT}(B) = \text{LEFT}(A)\{A\} \cup \text{LEFT}(A)$$

We can solve these equations by reversing the technique of Chapter 5, i.e. by rewriting the equations as a grammar. With each set we associate a nonterminal, $\hat{S}$ for LEFT(S), $\hat{A}$ for LEFT(A) and $\hat{B}$ for LEFT(B). The resulting grammar has nonterminals $\{\hat{S}, \hat{A}, \hat{B}\}$, terminals $\{A, [\}$ and non-redundant productions

$$\hat{S} \to \varepsilon$$
$$\hat{A} \to \hat{S} \mid \hat{B}[$$
$$\hat{B} \to \hat{A}A \mid \hat{A}$$

In general, the LEFT sets of a grammar $G = (N, T, P, S)$ can be derived from a grammar $\hat{G} = (\hat{N}, \hat{T}, \hat{P}, \hat{S})$ where $\hat{N} = \{\hat{A} \mid A \in N\}$ and $\hat{T} \subset N \cup T$. By the construction, the productions in $\hat{P}$ will be such that the grammar is *left-linear* and hence the LEFT sets are all regular (see Exercise 3.11). Thus, as a corollary of Theorem 8.2, we have the following theorem.

Theorem 8.3

For any CFG, $G = (N, T, P, S)$, the LRCONTEXT sets of productions in P are all regular sets.

This is a really exiting result! Regular sets are easy to handle and we can hope to exploit this in the design of a parser.

The construction of the FSA, $\hat{M}$, corresponding to the left-linear grammar $\hat{G}$ can be summarized as follows. For each production $\hat{A} \to \hat{B}x$, $\hat{A}$, $\hat{B} \in \hat{N}$, $x \in \hat{T}^*$ there is a path labelled x from a node labelled $\hat{B}$ to a node labelled $\hat{A}$ and for each production $\hat{A} \to x$, $A \in \hat{N}$, $x \in \hat{T}^*$ there is a path labelled x from the start state of $\hat{M}$ (which we will label 1) to the node labelled $\hat{A}$. Each path may comprise one or more arcs each labelled with elements of $\hat{T} \cup \{\varepsilon\}$. If a path comprises more than one arc then we will need to introduce special intermediate nodes (which we will label 2, 3, 4, etc.). If we denote the transition function of $\hat{M}$ by $\hat{t}$ then our construction will ensure that for all $A \in N$, LEFT(A) $= \{x \in \hat{T}^* \mid \hat{t}(1, x) = \hat{A}\}$.

The FSA constructed from our example is given in Fig. 8.2a.

From this we deduce that

$$\text{LEFT}(S) = 1$$
$$\text{LEFT}(A) = ((A + 1)[)^*$$
$$\text{LEFT}(B) = ((A + 1)[)^*(A + 1)$$

and hence that

$$\text{LRCONTEXT}(S \to A\$) = A\$$$
$$\text{LRCONTEXT}(A \to AB) = ((A + 1)[)^* AB$$

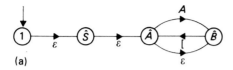

(a)

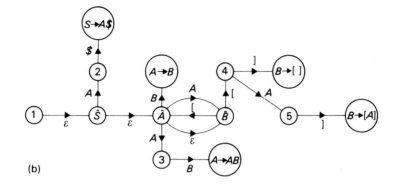

(b)

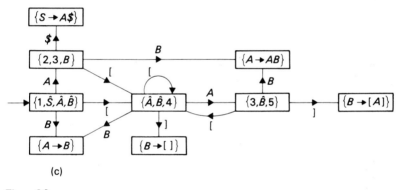

(c)

Figure 8.2

$$\text{LRCONTEXT}(A \to B) = ((A + 1)[)^* B$$
$$\text{LRCONTEXT}(B \to [A]) = ((A + 1)[)^*(A + 1)[A]$$
$$\text{LRCONTEXT}(B \to []) = ((A + 1)[)^*(A + 1)[]$$

From Theorem 8.1, we can see that G_3 is indeed $LR(0)$.

Once the FSA $\hat{M}$ is constructed, we can use Theorem 8.2 to construct another FSA which contains a state corresponding to each production of the original grammar and such that the set of strings which lead us from the start state of this FSA to a state labelled with some production is exactly the LRCONTEXT set for that production. For our example, we obtain the FSA of Fig. 8.2b. The equivalent deterministic FSA with no ε-productions is given in Fig. 8.2c. Such an automaton is known as the *characteristic*

Table 8.4

Step	Prefix of sentential form input to characteristic automaton	Remaining input = remaining part of the sentential form	Reduction applied	new sentential form
1	[[]	[]][]$	$B \to$ []	[B[]][]$
2	[B	[]][]$	$A \to B$	[A[]][]$
3	[A[]	][]$	$B \to$ []	[AB][]$
4	[AB	][]$	$A \to AB$	[A][]$
5	[A]	[]$	$B \to$ [A]	B[]$
6	B	[]$	$A \to B$	A[]$
7	A[]	$	$B \to$ []	AB$
8	AB	$	$A \to AB$	A$
9	A$	ε	$S \to AS$	S

automaton for the grammar. The nodes of a characteristic automaton which contain a production in its label are called *reducing states*. A grammar is *LR*(0) iff the reducing states of its characteristic automaton are each labelled with only one production and have no exits labelled by terminal symbols.

Let us see how we can use our example characteristic automaton to verify that [[][]][]$ is in the language. We input the string to the automaton, one character at a time, until we obtain a reducing state. This tells us which reduction to apply and thus we get another (rightmost) sentential form. Again, we can find which reduction is appropriate by inputing a prefix of this sentential form to the characteristic automaton. The repeated use of this approach yields the steps tabulated in Table 8.4.

This is not a very efficient use of the characteristic automaton. We are doing an unnecessary amount of work by re-entering the automaton after each reduction. For example, in step 4, we have just reduced [] to B. Now, if in the previous step we had remembered that we were in state $\{3, \hat{B}, 5\}$ after we had processed [A and before we processed [], we could then deduce that an input of [AB would result in the state $t(\{3, \hat{B}, 5\}, B)$. Before we pursue this, let us simplify discussion by renaming the states of the characteristic automaton, $1, 2, \ldots$ where 1 is the start state and we remember which states are reducing states in an associated *reducing table*. If state k is a reducing state with associated production $A \to \beta$ (say), then the kth entry of the reducing table is set to $A \to \beta$. A suitable relabelling of the states of our characteristic automaton and its associated reducing table is given in Fig. 8.3.

We can now design an efficient parsing algorithm using a stack of states. At each step of our algorithm, this stack will contain the states through which the characteristic automaton would have passed had we input the

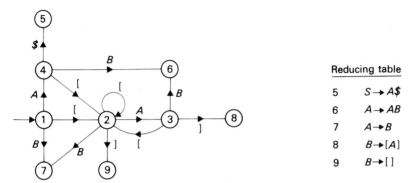

Reducing table	
5	$S \to A\$$
6	$A \to AB$
7	$A \to B$
8	$B \to [A]$
9	$B \to [ ]$

Figure 8.3

current prefix of the right sentential form. For example, if the current prefix is $[A[]$ the stack will contain $1, 2, 3, 2, 9$ (listed from the bottom to the top). At each stage, there are four possible moves:

(a) *reduction move*: if the top stack symbol, k, is a reducing state with associated production $A \to X_1 X_2 \ldots X_m$ say and $A \neq S$, then, if the stack contents is $1 = k_0, k_1, \ldots, k_n = k (n \geq m)$, we reduce using the production $A \to X_1 X_2 \ldots X_m$, pop the top m states off the stack and push $t(k_{n-m}, A)$

(b) *shift move*: if the top stack symbol, k, is not a reducing state, we perform a shift reading $a \in T$ (say) from the input stream and the state $t(k, a)$ is pushed onto the stack.

Table 8.5

Stack	Move
1	shift [
1, 2	shift [
1, 2, 2	shift]
1, 2, 2, 9	reduce using $B \to [ ]$
1, 2, 7	reduce using $A \to B$
1, 2, 3	shift [
1, 2, 3, 2	shift]
1, 2, 3, 2, 9	reduce using $B \to [ ]$
1, 2, 3, 6	reduce using $A \to AB$
1, 2, 3	shift]
1, 2, 3, 8	reduce using $B \to [A]$
1, 7	reduce using $A \to B$
1, 4	Shift [
1, 4, 2	shift]
1, 4, 2, 9	reduce using $B \to [ ]$
1, 4, 6	reduce using $A \to AB$
1, 4	shift $\$$
1, 4, 5	accept.

(c) *accept move*: if the top stack symbol is a reducing state corresponding to the unique production with S on the lefthand side, $S \to \alpha$ (say), then provided there are only $|\alpha| + 1$ states on the stack, the algorithm halts in an accept state.

(d) *fail move*: if none of the above moves is possible, there is an error in the input and either the algorithm halts or some attempt at a repair is made.

Using our relabelled automaton, the stack contents for a parse of $[[\,][\,]]\$$ changes as tabulated in Table 8.5

If a grammar is $LR(0)$ then it is possible to automate the construction of the corresponding characteristic automaton. Once this is achieved, the compiler writer can easily construct a parser for the language. Unfortunately, it is rare for a grammar to satisfy the $LR(0)$ condition but, luckily, LR parsing can be generalized in a variety of ways to yield truly powerful techniques.

LR(1) GRAMMARS

Consider the grammar, G_4, with productions

$$S \to E\$$$
$$E \to E + T \mid T$$
$$T \to T \times F \mid F$$
$$F \to a \mid (E)$$

Reduction table

3	$T \to F$
4	$F \to a$
6	$E \to T$
7	$S \to E\$$
11	$E \to E + T$
12	$F \to (E)$
13	$T \to T \times F$

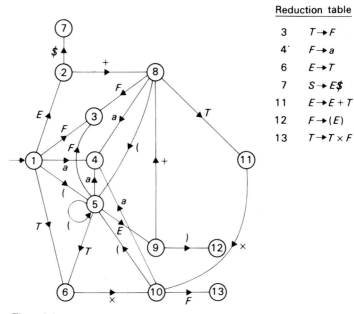

Figure 8.4

The characteristic automaton for G_4 is given in Fig. 8.4. From this we see that G_4 is not $LR(0)$, for example, $T \in \text{LRCONTEXT}(E \to T)$ but $T \times a \in \text{LRCONTEXT}(F \to a)$ and $T \times F \in \text{LRCONTEXT}(T \to T \times F)$. Thus, if the current stack contents is 1,6 then we do not know whether to perform a shift or a reduction move. In this case, we can resolve this dilemma by using a one-symbol lookahead. If the next incoming symbol is $\times$ we must execute a shift but if not, we need a reduction. G_4 is an example of what is called an $LR(1)$ grammar—for such grammars we can modify the LR parser which we have described to resolve conflicts in the characteristic automaton by using a one symbol lookahead. In general, if a grammar is $LR(k)$ (some integer $k \geq 0$) then conflicts in its characteristic automaton can always be resolved using a k symbol lookahead. In practice, the case $k = 1$ is by far the most important and we will thus concentrate on this—the generalization of the argument to an arbitrary k follows very similar reasoning.

Let $G = (N, T, P, S)$ be an arbitrary grammar which we will assume has already been augmented in the usual way by the addition of a special end-of-input marker, $\$$. Thus the only production in P which involves S is of the form $S \to E\$$ for some $E \in N$. We define the $LR(1)\text{CONTEXT}$ set of a production $A \to \beta$ in P by

$$\text{LR}(1)\text{CONTEXT}(A \to \beta) = \{\alpha \mid \alpha = \gamma\beta a \in (N \cup T)^* T \text{ where } S \overset{*}{\Rightarrow} \\ \gamma A a x \Rightarrow \gamma\beta a x \text{ is a rightmost production} \\ \text{for some } a \in T, \ x \in T^*, \ \gamma \in (N \cup T)^*\}.$$

If $\alpha \in \text{LR}(1)\text{CONTEXT}(A \to \beta)$ then $\alpha = \alpha' a$ for some $\alpha' \in \text{LRCONTEXT}(A \to \beta)$ and $a \in T$. The $a \in T$ is the one symbol lookahead which we wish to incorporate into our parser. Generalizing Theorem 8.1, we make the following definition.

Let $G = (N, T, P, S)$ be an augmented CFG. G is said to be an $LR(1)$ *grammar* iff

if $\alpha \in \text{LR}(1)\text{CONTEXT}(A \to \beta)$ and $\alpha x \in \text{LR}(1)\text{CONTEXT}(B \to \beta')$ where $A \to \beta$, $B \to \beta' \in P$, $\alpha \in (N \cup T)^*$ and $x \in T^*$, then $x = \varepsilon$, $A = B$ and $\beta = \beta'$.

Thus, to test if a grammar is or is not $LR(1)$ we need to compute the $\text{LR}(1)\text{CONTEXT}$ sets of each of its productions. Let $A \in N$ and $a \in \text{FOLLOW}(A)$, we define

$$\text{LEFT}_1(A, a) = \{\gamma \mid S \overset{*}{\Rightarrow} \gamma A a x \text{ is a rightmost derivation}, x \in T^*\}.$$

It then follows that

$$\text{LR}(1)\text{CONTEXT}(A \to \beta) = \bigcup_{a \in \text{FOLLOW}(A)} \text{LEFT}_1(A, a) \cdot \{\beta a\}.$$

Now, we need to compute all the LEFT_1 sets. We do this in a similar way to the one we used to compute LEFT sets. Firstly, we observe that if $B \to \gamma_1 A \gamma_2$ is a production of G, $b \in \text{FOLLOW}(B)$ and $a \in \{\text{FIRST}(x) | \gamma_2 b \stackrel{*}{\Rightarrow} x\}$ then clearly $a \in \text{FOLLOW}(A)$ and $\text{LEFT}_1(A, a) \supset \text{LEFT}_1(B, b) \cdot \{\gamma_1\}$. This leads to a set of equations for the LEFT_1 sets and as with the LEFT sets these equations correspond to a left-linear grammar. The LEFT_1 sets are thus all regular and hence so are the $LR(1) \text{CONTEXT}$ sets. From the grammar defining the LEFT_1 sets, we can construct a DFSA defining the $LR(1)$ CONTEXT sets. Analogously to the characteristic automaton for $LR(0)$ grammars, provided the grammar is $LR(1)$ we can use this DFSA to produce our bottom-up parser. Unfortunately, this DFSA tends to have a large number of states and its construction can be a laborious task. Rather than calculate the $LR(1) \text{CONTEXT}$ sets in this way, it is sometimes possible to prove an (augmented) grammar is $LR(1)$ by proving a stronger condition known as the *simple LR(1)* condition. We define the simple $LR(1)$ context of the production $A \to \beta$ in the grammar by

$$\text{SLR}(1)\,\text{CONTEXT}\,(A \to \beta) = \text{LRCONTEXT}\,(A \to \beta) \cdot \text{FOLLOW}\,(A)$$

Thus, by definition, the $LR(1)$ CONTEXT set of a production is a subset of its $SLR(1)$ CONTEXT set.

We define an (augmented) grammar, $G = (N, T, P, S)$, to be a *simple LR(1) grammar* (often abbreviated to *SLR(1) grammar*) iff

> if $\alpha \in \text{SLR}(1)\text{CONTEXT}(A \to \beta)$ and $\alpha x \in \text{SLR}(1)\text{CONTEXT} \cdot (B \to \beta')$ where $A \to \beta$ and $B \to \beta' \in P$, $\alpha \in (N \cup T)^*$ and $x \in T^*$ then $x = \varepsilon$, $A = B$ and $\beta = \beta'$.

An immediate corollary of these definitions is that

Theorem 8.4

Every *SLR(1)* grammar is *LR(1)*.

However, the converse is not true (see Exercise 8.5). Now, G_4 is SLR(1). The FOLLOW sets can be easily computed using the techniques of Chapter 7.

> $\text{FOLLOW}(S) = \varnothing$
> $\text{FOLLOW}(E) = \{ +,), \$ \}$
> $\text{FOLLOW}(T) = \{ \times, +,), \$ \}$
> $\text{FOLLOW}(F) = \{ \times, +,), \$ \}$

Hence, by referring to the characteristic automaton of Fig. 8.4, it is clear that the SLR(1) CONTEXT sets satisfy the conditions required for the

Table 8.6

Stack	Move
1	shift a
1,4	reduce using $F \to a$
1,3	reduce using $T \to F$
1,6	(use one-symbol lookahead to determine) reduce using $E \to T$
1,2	shift $+$
1,2,8	shift a
1,2,8,4	reduce using $F \to a$
1,2,8,3	reduce using $T \to F$
1,2,8,11	(use one-symbol lookahead to determine) shift $\times$
1,2,8,11,10	shift a
1,2,8,11,10,4	reduce using $F \to a$
1,2,8,11,10,13	reduce using $T \to T \times F$
1,2,8,11	(use one-symbol lookahead to determine) reduce using $E \to E + T$
1,2	shift $+$
1,2,8	shift a
1,2,8,4	reduce using $F \to a$
1,2,8,3	reduce using $T \to F$
1,2,8,11	(use one-symbol lookahead to determine) reduce using $E \to E + T$
1,2	shift $\$$
1,2,7	accept.

grammar to be SLR(1). We can now design an LR parser for G_4 based upon this observation. We know that any conflicts arising from the use of the characteristic automaton can be resolved by a one-symbol lookahead. We will illustrate this by parsing $a + a \times a + a\$$—see Table 8.6.

Now, an LR parser tells us in which order the reductions are to be made and thus implicitly generates a derivation tree. If we wish to embed semantic actions in our parser, then this is generally not too difficult. Say we wished to generate semantic trees corresponding to the arithmetic expressions generated by G_4. One technique would be to associate with each element, X, of the current prefix of the sentential form, a tree T_X. T_X is the semantic tree corresponding to the part of the derivation tree which is rooted at X. Whenever we shift a symbol $a \in T$, we are adding it to the current prefix and we associate with this new symbol the tree, T_a, comprising just one node, @. Then, whenever we apply a reduction $A \to X_1 X_2 \ldots X_k$, we replace the right-most occurrence of $X_1 X_2 \ldots X_k$ in the

Table 8.7

Reduction	Semantic rule
$S \to E\$$	$T_S := T_E$
$E \to E + T$	$T_E := tree\ construct\ (+, T_E, T_T)$
$E \to T$	$T_E := T_T$
$T \to T \times F$	$T_T := tree\ construct\ (\times, T_T, T_F)$
$T \to F$	$T_T := T_F$
$F \to a$	$T_F := T_a$
$F \to (E)$	$T_F := T_E$

current prefix by A. Associated with the reduction is a *semantic rule* describing how the trees $T_{X_1}, T_{X_2}, \ldots, T_{X_k}$ are combined to form the tree T_A. Any successful parse will eventually result in an accept state with current prefix, S, and the desired associated semantic tree, T_S.

The semantic rules associated with the productions of G_4 are easy to construct and are given in Table 8.7.

THEORETICAL CONSIDERATIONS

The LR parsing technique is theoretically superior to the LL technique since any (augmented) $LL(k)$ grammar has been shown to be $LR(k)$. However, there are grammars that are $LL(1)$ but not $SLR(1)$ (see Exercise 8.6). Every $LR(k)$ grammar necessarily defines a deterministic language but also every deterministic language can be defined by an $LR(1)$ grammar. Thus, a language is generated by an $LR(k)$ grammar iff it is generated by an $LR(1)$ grammar. The $LR(0)$ grammars define exactly those deterministic languages which satisfy the *prefix property*, i.e. whenever x is in L no proper prefix of x is in L. Thus, if we use an end-of-input marker, $\$$, every deterministic language $L\$$ satisfies the prefix property and hence can be generated by an $LR(0)$ grammar. In practice, the compiler writer will usually be satisfied with an $LR(1)$ grammar or preferably one of its simple variants such as $SLR(1)$. For a full theoretical discussion and proof of these results, the reader is referred to *Formal Languages and their Relation to Automata* by J.E. Hopcroft and J.D. Ullman (Addison-Wesley) and *Syntax of Programming Languages: Theory and Practice* by R.C. Backhouse (Prentice-Hall). For a more practical approach to LR parsing techniques, a good text is *Principles of Computer Design* by A.V. Aho and J.D. Ullman (Addison-Wesley) where the variation of LR grammars known as $LALR$ grammars is discussed.

EXERCISES

1 Let $G = (N, T, P, S)$ be an arbitrary CFG and define the relations F and L on $N \cup T$ by

XFY iff there exists a production in P of the form $X \to Y\gamma, \gamma \in (N \cup T)^*$,

and

XLY iff there exists a production in P of the form $X \to \gamma Y, \gamma \in (N \cup T)^*$.

If R^+, R^* and R^{-1} respectively denotes the transitive closure of a relation R, the reflexive closure of the transitive closure of R and the inverse of R, show that

$$(<\cdot) = (\doteq)_{\circ}(F^+)$$

and

$$(\cdot>) = (L^+)^{-1}(\doteq)\ (F^*)$$

(The relations $\doteq$, F and L are easily computed. F^+ and L^+ can then be computed using Warshall's algorithm, published in JACM 9, 11–12, January 1962. $F^* = F^+ \cup I$ where I is the identity relation. These results thus give us a method of computing the relations $<\cdot$ and $\cdot>$.)

2 Compute the precedence relations for the grammar

$$S \to A\$$$
$$A \to aABC \mid CB$$
$$B \to aB \mid C$$
$$C \to b$$

Is this grammar a simple precedence grammar?

3 Show that the grammar of Exercise 8.2 is $LR(0)$ by computing its characteristic automaton

4 Show that the grammar

$$S \to A$$
$$A \to Ab \mid bBa$$
$$B \to aAc \mid a \mid aAb$$

is not $LR(0)$ but is $SLR(1)$.

5 Let $G = (N, T, P, S)$ be an arbitrary CFG and k a positive integer. Assume G has been augmented to ensure that there are k end-of-input markers, $\$$, at the end of each string in $L(G)$. Define

$$\text{FOLLOW}_k(A) = \{x \mid \text{length}(x) = k \text{ and } S \overset{*}{\Rightarrow} y_1 A x y_2 \text{ for some } y_1, y_2 \in T^*\}.$$

The SLR(k) CONTEXT set of a production $A \to \beta$ in G is then defined by

$$\text{SLR}(k)\,\text{CONTEXT}(A \to \beta) = \text{LRCONTEXT}\,(A \to \beta)\cdot \text{FOLLOW}_k(A).$$

Use this definition to formally define an SLR(k) grammar and hence show that

$$S \to A\$$$
$$A \to BaCD$$
$$B \to b$$
$$C \to B \mid Ea$$
$$D \to ba \mid Dba$$
$$E \to b$$

is $LR(1)$ but not $SLR(k)$ for any $k > 0$.

6 Show that the grammar

$$S \to A\$$$
$$A \to BaBb \mid CbCa$$
$$B \to \varepsilon$$
$$C \to \varepsilon$$

is $LL(1)$ but not $SLR(1)$.

7 Generalize the definition of an $LR(1)$ grammar to that of an $LR(k)$ grammar.

8 Write a PASCAL program to implement an LR parser for simple arithmetic expressions. Your program should accept valid arithmetic expressions over the variables $\{a, b, c, \ldots, z\}$ and deliver the corresponding semantic trees. Any invalid expressions should be reported as such.

Index

accept move   114
accepted by DFSA   35
  by DPDA   79
  by NFSA   37
  by NPDA   72
acceptor   74
  see FSA, PDA
Aho, A.V.   118
ALGOL   99
algorithm   52
algorithms for context-free grammars   56,
  60–62
  for regular grammars   52–53
  for transitive closure   119
alphabet   11
ambiguous grammar   22
ancestor   11
arc   10
arithmetic expressions   23–25, 75–76,
  96–99, 114, 116
associative   3
augmented grammar   90
automaton
  see FSA, PDA

Backhouse, R.C.   99
Backus-Naur Form
  see BNF
backtracking   85
bijection   8
blank   11
BNF   xii, 16–17, 29
bottom of stack   70
bottom-up parsing   85, 102–120

Cantor's diagonalization   5
cardinality   5
CFG   20–28, 55–69
  see PDA
CFL   20–28, 55–69
  see PDA
characteristic automaton   111
child   11
Chomsky Normal Form   57–58

closure of languages   12
  of relations   8
  of strings   12
closure properties   83
commutative   3
complement of a CFL   69, 83
  of a DCFL   82–83
  of a regular language   40–41, 83
  of a set   3
composition   13
concatenation of CFLs   68, 83
  of DCFLs   83
  of languages   12
  of regular languages   31–33, 83
  of sets   12
  of strings   11
configuration   72
context-free grammar
  see CFG
context-free language
  see CFL
countable   5–6, 9

Davie, A.J.T.   99
DCFL   79–83
De Morgan's laws   4
defining property   2
depth of a node   13
  of a tree   13
derivation   19–20
  problem   62
  tree   21
descendant   11
deterministic CFL   79–83
  FSA   34–36, 38
  PDA   79–83
DFSA   34–36, 38
diagonalization   5
difference   3
digraph   9
directed graph   9
disjoint sets   5
  graphs   10
distributivity   4
domain   6

DPDA 79–83

element 1
emptiness problem 52–53, 55–56
empty function 91
  set 2
  stack 70
  store 83
  string 11, 25–27, 41–43
epsilon 11, 25–27, 41–43
  -free 25–27
  -generating 25
  -moves 41
  -productions 25
  -reachable 41
equivalence class 7
  problem 53
  relation 7
equivalent grammars 20
Even, S. 83
external node 10

fail move 114
final state 34, 71
finite automaton
  see FSA
finite set 5
finiteness problem 53, 61–62
FIRST 91
FIRST 87
fixed point theorem 67
FOLLOW 91
FOLLOW 119
formal language 12
Foster's Syntax Improving Device 90
FSA 33–54, 73, 78–79, 110–112
function 8

generated 20
grammar
  see regular grammar, CFG
Greibach Normal Form 63–66

halt node state 33
handle 102
homomorphism 44, 69, 83
Hopcroft, J.E. xii, 118

idempotence 4
index 49
indistinguishable 49
infinite 5
inherently ambiguous 27
input alphabet 34, 71
internal node 11
intersection of CFLs 69
  of DCFLs 83–84

of regular languages 41
of sets 3
with regular languages 78, 83
involution 4
irrelevant productions 56–57

k-LOOKAHEAD 100
Kleene closure 12, 31, 45, 68, 83
Kleene's theorem 48
Knuth, D.E. 107

LALR grammar 118
language 12, 20
leaf node 10
LEFT 109
LEFT₁ 115
left-linear 44
left-recursive 63
leftmost derivation 22
length 11
lexical analysis 29
LL(l) grammar 88–94, 99–100
LL(k) grammar 86–100, 118
LOOKAHEAD 91
LR(0) grammar 107–114
LR(l) grammar 114–118
LR(k) grammar 115, 118
LRCONTEXT 108
LR(1)CONTEXT 115

machine
  see FSA, PDA
machine code 23
membership problem 40, 62, 68
MIN(L) 84
minimal DFSA 48–52
monotonic increasing 14, 67
Morrison, R. 99
Myhill–Nerode theorem 50

nextsymbol 95
NFSA 36–43
node 9
non-CFL 60
nondeterministic
  see NFSA, NPDA
nonterminal 16, 18
NPDA 71–78

one–one 8
onto 8
overflow 70

pair 5

parse tree 21
partial derivation tree 56
  function 8
PASCAL 15, 28, 90
path 10
PDA 70–84
phrase structure grammar 18
POP 70
postfix 12
power set 13
precedence function 106
  see simple precedence
Pref 43
prefix 12
prefix property 118
product of sets 6
production 18
properties of languages 83
  of sets 4
PSG 18
pumping lemma for CFGs 59
  for regular grammars 52
PUSH 70
pushdown function 70
pushdown automaton 70–84

range 6
recursive descent 94–99
reduction 102, 105, 112–113
reflexive relation 7
  closure 8, 119
regular espression 45–48
  grammar 30–54
  language/set 30–54, 110
  see intersection with regular language
relation 6, 49
reversal 13
right invariant 49
right-linear 44
right-recursive 69
rightmost derivation 102

scanner 29
secondary productions 57
semantic actions 95
  rule 118
  tree 23
semantics xii
sentence 20
sentential form 19
set 1–9
set equations 67
shift 105, 113
  see PUSH
shift-reduce parsers 105
SID 90
simple LR(l) 116

LR(k) 119
  precedence 103–107
singleton set 5
SLR(l) 116
SLR(k) 119
SLR(l)CONTEXT 116
SLR(k)CONTEXT 119
solvable 52
stack 70, 83, 94, 105–107, 112–114, 117
stack automaton
  see PDA
start state 34, 71
  symbol 18
state 34, 71
Stearns, R.E. 89
string 11–12
strong LL(k) 87–89
subset 2
substring 12
symmetric closure 8
  relation 7
syntax xi
  charts 15–16, 97
system of set equations 67–68
terminal symbol 16, 18
tertiary production 57
tip node 10
T(M) 35, 37, 72
top-down parsing 85, 102–120
total function 8
transition array 35
  function 34
transitive closure 8
  relation 7
tree 10
  see derivation tree, semantic tree
treeconstruct 98

Ullman, J.D. xiii, 118
unambiguous 88, 100
underflow 70
union of CFLs 68
  of DCFLs 83–84
  of regular languages 31
  of sets 3
unit production 57
universe 2
unsolvable 93
uvwxy theorem 59

variable
  see nonterminal
vertex 9

Warshall's algorithm 118
word
  see string